POLITICAL PROFILES
BARACK OBAMA

Political Profiles
Barack Obama

Kerrily Sapet

MORGAN
REYNOLDS
PUBLISHING

Greensboro, North Carolina

POLITICAL PROFILES

Barack Obama
Hillary Clinton
John McCain
Nancy Pelosi
Al Gore
Rudy Giuliani
Arnold Schwarzenegger

POLITICAL PROFILES: BARACK OBAMA
Copyright © 2008 by Kerrily Sapet

Library of Congress Cataloging-in-Publication Data

Sapet, Kerrily, 1972-
  Political profiles : Barack Obama / by Kerrily Sapet.
    p. cm.
  Includes bibliographical references and index.
  ISBN-13: 978-1-59935-045-5
  ISBN-10: 1-59935-045-9
    1. Obama, Barack--Juvenile literature. 2. Legislators--United States--
Biography--Juvenile literature. 3. African American legislators--Biography-
-Juvenile literature. 4. United States. Congress. Senate--Biography--Juvenile
literature. 5. Presidential candidates--United States--Biography--Juvenile
literature. 6. Racially mixed people--United States--Biography--Juvenile lit-
erature. I. Title.
  E901.1.O23S27 2007
  328.73092--dc22
  [B]
                                                 2007018657

Printed in the United States of America
First Edition

To my son Benjamin, who is already
a writer and a weaver of words

Contents

Barack Obama
(Courtesy AP Images)

one
A Window to the World

As a young boy living on the Hawaiian island of Oahu, Barack Obama swam and body surfed in the gleaming azure waters. Volcanic peaks and craters towered in the distance, edging the wide, white sand beaches. The days glazed him in golden sunshine as he snacked on roast pig, sliced raw fish called sashimi, and rice candy with edible wrappers. Barack was a skinny kid with big ears and a funny name. It seemed impossible that one day he would be the United States senator from Illinois and would run for president.

Barack Hussein Obama was born on August 4, 1961, in Hawaii's capital city of Honolulu. In Swahili, his name means "Blessed by God," in Hebrew it means "flash of lightning." Barack's mother, Stanley Ann Dunham, was a white woman from Kansas, the heartland of the United States. His father, also named Barack Obama, was from Kenya, a country on the east coast of Africa. The couple's geographically and ethnically different backgrounds would one day lead their son to quip, "My name comes from Kenya, and my accent comes from Kansas."

Barack's mother's ancestors hailed from Scotland, Ireland, Kansas, and the Cherokee Indian lands. Born in Wichita, Kansas in the years after World War II, Stanley Ann Dunham was named after her father, who had wanted a son. Her mother, Madelyn, had manned the home front, working in a factory during the war, while her father had served in George S. Patton's army, which fought across Europe.

Stanley had been teased for her boyish name. After enduring nicknames such as "Stan the Man" and "Stanley Steamer," she dropped the Stanley and decided to go by Ann. Many of the families around her worked for the local oil company or farmed corn like her father. But Ann's father, always seeking better employment, moved the family around the country, changing jobs frequently.

After Ann finished high school, she and her family moved to Hawaii, where her father took a job at a furniture store. Hawaii, soon to become the fiftieth state on August 21, 1959, was a chain of nineteen islands. Formed by volcanic activity, the islands are the exposed peaks of an undersea mountain range. For the Dunhams, the idea of opportunity, combined with bright sunshine and crystal beaches, was too appealing to pass up.

The family settled in Honolulu, on the southeast coast of Oahu, one of Hawaii's main islands. From their house, framed by a large Chinese banyan tree and monkey pod tree, they could see Diamond Head crater in the distance surrounded by the indigo waters. The Dunhams mingled with their neighbors, who represented a mix of cultures and different

A photograph of Honolulu taken in 1961 *(Courtesy of AP Images)*

nationalities. At age eighteen, Ann enrolled in the University of Hawaii. During her first year, in a Russian language class, she met a tall, foreign student and fell in love.

Barack Obama was of the Luo people of Kenya. The Luo, sometimes called Joluo, live along the banks of Lake Victoria and other areas of Africa, and are the third largest community in Kenya. According to the Luo, they were led from present day Uganda into Kenya by the warrior chief Ramogi Ajwang about five hundred years ago.

Obama had grown up in a poor village along Lake Victoria, herding his family's goats. In the plains, nearby leopards, elephants, gazelles, rhinoceros, and lions roamed, and hippos cooled themselves in pools. The Luo tribe held Obama's father, Hussein Onyango Obama, in high esteem. He was the tribal elder and healer. After being abandoned by his mother at nine years old, Obama was raised by his stepmother, Sarah Hussein Onyango. He attended a school set up by the British government that ruled Kenya as a colony. In this tin-roofed shack, he began to learn English, in addition to his native language of Dholuo.

A quick learner, Obama earned a scholarship to attend a better school in Nairobi, the capital of Kenya. As he studied, Kenya gained its independence from Britain and Kenyan leaders established a joint education program with the United States. The country sent its most promising students to universities in the U.S. The students then returned to Kenya, using their new knowledge to help the country become a modern nation.

In 1959, Obama was chosen to attend the University of Hawaii. At age twenty-three he became the school's first African student. He studied economics, received top grades, and formed the International Students' Association.

Ann and Obama were drawn to each other by their love of debate, diversity, and a deep sense of justice. They had much to talk about. Racial protests had broken out across the country. In many southern states, laws separated black and white people in nearly every aspect of public life, from schools to bathrooms to restaurants to theaters. Signs indicating separate black and white facilities dotted towns and cities. Black people were relegated to subservient positions

Prejudice, segregation, and discrimination were common in areas of the United States during the early sixties. *(Library of Congress)*

and forced to accept lesser work for lesser pay. When Ann invited Obama home, her parents were unsure whether such a relationship could withstand racial prejudices. But Obama's intelligence and charm won them over.

When the couple decided to marry, Obama's father wrote him a long letter. He also wrote to Ann's father detailing why the pair should not marry. He didn't think Obama was acting responsibly because he already had a Kenyan wife, named Kezia, who had given birth to two children, Roy and Auma. However, according to Luo custom, a man could marry more than one woman, as long as he supported his wives and their children. But Obama's father questioned whether Ann would return and live as a Luo, and whether she would accept the fact that her husband had a second family.

Despite their parents' concerns, Ann and Obama married in 1960. Their marriage represented a bold move at the time. Half of the states in the U.S. banned racially mixed marriages. Obama could be hanged if they traveled together as a married couple in the southern states.

Together, they lived with Ann's parents until they finished school. A year later their son Barack was born. They nicknamed him Barry. After Barry was born, Ann began working as a secretary. Two years later, Barry's father graduated at the top of his class. He had completed a four-year program in three years. He planned for his new family to return to Kenya, but both Harvard University in Boston and the New

A young Obama with his mother, Ann (*Courtesy of Polaris Images*)

School in New York City offered him a scholarship. The scholarship from the New School came with a campus job, room and board, and enough money to support the three of them. But the prestige of Harvard was too difficult to pass up, even though the money covered only one student. Ann and Barry stayed behind in Hawaii. Gradually, time and distance eroded the relationship, and Barry's parents divorced.

After attending Harvard, Barry's father, now Dr. Obama, returned to Kenya. He took a white woman named Ruth, who he had met in Boston, back to Kenya with him. His Luo family had been expecting Ann and Barry. However, Obama and Ruth married shortly after arriving in Kenya.

After the divorce, Ann's parents began to play a bigger role in Barry's upbringing. His name for his grandfather was Gramps. Madelyn, his grandmother, he called Toot, a shortened version of *Tutu,* the Hawaiian word for grandmother. Gramps took him to see astronauts landing at nearby Hickam Air Force base. They went spearfishing in the glistening, clear waters of Kailua Bay, and spent time swimming in the sparkling waters of Sandy Beach, at the base of the Koko volcanic crater.

Growing up in Hawaii in the 1960s, Barry lived among a group of diverse nationalities and ethnic groups and grew to respect other cultures. Like Gramps and Toot, many people living in Hawaii had roots in the United States. Others, though, came from Japan, China, and the Philippines. The bustling capital of Honolulu illustrated that international mix. The words *Hono* meant "a joining together," and *lulu* meant "a shelter from the wind." The city's nickname was The Gathering Place.

When Barry was six years old, his mother remarried. Lolo Soetoro, an Indonesian student studying at the University of Hawaii, had thick dark hair and a gentle smile. With his easygoing manner, Soetoro made time to wrestle with Barry and play chess with Gramps. After Ann's marriage to Soetoro, she and Barry moved to Djakarta, the capital of Indonesia.

Indonesia is a nation of more than 17,000 islands stretching across the Indian and Pacific Oceans along the equator. Many Indonesians live on the islands of Java, Sumatra, Bali, Sulawesi, and New Guinea. In 1965, shortly before the family's move to Indonesia, an Indonesian military leader, General Suharto, had instituted a bloody rebellion against the government led by Sukarno, the country's first leader since Indonesia had won its independence from the Netherlands. Between 500,000 and 1 million people were killed, and more

During his time in Indonesia, Obama lived on the outskirts of the capital city, Djakarta.

than 700,000 either fled the country or were imprisoned. Suharto eventually overthrew Sukarno. News of the violence in this faraway corner of the world was slow to reach newspapers in the United States, so Barry's mother had no idea of the country's upheaval when she and Barry traveled in Indonesia in 1967, the same year Suharto assumed the presidency.

When Barry and his mother arrived in Djakarta, they passed small villages and saw boys riding water buffalo into a brown river. Tiny stores and small white houses dotted the sides of the dirt road. They stopped when they came to Soetoro's house, the first house at the edge of town. Barry had gone from a home in a big city to a small open house bordering the jungle. The backyard fenced in chickens, ducks, and a large tan dog. The menagerie of animals also included two plumed birds of paradise, a white cockatoo, two baby crocodiles, and a pet gibbon named Tata. Barry watched as Soetoro's servant lopped the head off a chicken for their welcome dinner. That night he fell asleep under a mosquito net to the tune of the chirping crickets. To the young boy, the move was a great adventure. "I could hardly believe my good fortune," he wrote.

Soon Soetoro began working as a geologist, and Ann took a job teaching English at the American Embassy. Soetoro treated Barry like his son. He introduced him to local dishes, such as dog meat, snake meat, and roasted grasshopper. They ate small green raw chilies with dinner, along with plenty of rice. Soetoro promised he'd bring home a piece of tiger meat for Barry to try. He also taught him about Islam, animal powers, and how to deal with Djakarta's endless stream of street beggars. After Barry came home bruised following a fight, Soetoro also taught him how to defend himself.

Djakarta was a jumble of streets, packed with a few cars, motorcycles, carts, and *becak,* or transport bikes. The areas around Barry's new home flooded waist-deep during rainy seasons. Other times droughts and the beating sun scorched the fields of rice and cassava, drying them to dust.

Barry focused on playing with other kids and exploring. He walked through rice paddies and felt the packed mud beneath his feet. Any inconveniences in his new home, such as the cold baths, the constant battle against biting mosquitoes, or the hole in the ground serving as a toilet, didn't bother him. Barry would vividly remember watching the sun rise behind the mountain peaks, smelling wood smoke in the air, and seeing musicians' faces lit by flickering firelight.

At the time, Barry saw his family as well off. They always had enough to eat, unlike many others in the area. The divisions between rich and poor were visible everywhere; disease and poverty plagued many people. Fortunately, the embassy paid his mother in dollars, not in the local *rupiahs.* Sometimes she took Barry to the American Club, where he jumped in the refreshing pool and sipped Coca-Cola. When Barry invited friends over to play, they looked at the pictures his grandparents had sent of Walt Disney World and the Empire State Building. But Barry's ties to the United States made him different, and neighborhood kids sometimes made fun of him.

Barry's mother and stepfather couldn't afford to send him to a private school. For a year he attended the local school, along with the children of neighboring farmers and servants. Barry liked to sit in the back and doodle cartoon superheroes, like

Spiderman and Batman. Despite his differences, and the teasing he endured at times, Barry was considerate to others.

"He would be very helpful with friends," said Barry's first grade teacher, Israella Pareira Darmawan. "He'd pick them up if they fell down. He would protect the smaller ones."

Soon after, Barry switched to the Besuki School, which he attended for three years. The Besuki School, although in a Muslim country, recognized several different religions, including Christianity and Hinduism. He once got into trouble for making faces during a class about the Koran. Years later, amidst rising fears of radical Islamic religious schools called madrasas, which sometimes mix religious instruction with political hatred of non-Muslim cultures, Barry's political critics would falsely contend that the Besuki School was a madrasa.

Barry had not been raised in a religious household. His mother believed that organized religion was closed minded, but she provided her son with some instruction on world religions. The Bible, the Koran, and the Hindu Bhagavad-Gita rested on their bookshelves, alongside Greek, Norse, and African mythology. She had taken Barry to church on Christmas and Easter, but had also gone to Buddhist temples, Shinto shrines, ancient Hawaiian burial sites, and Chinese New Year celebrations.

Even so, she was more concerned with her son learning the multiplication tables than religious lessons. To Barry's mother, his current education wasn't enough. At times he struggled with the Indonesian language, making learning difficult. His mother worried that the education he was receiving might limit his opportunities. She ordered teaching supplies from the United States and set to work providing additional schooling for her son. She woke Barry at four o'clock in the morning each day. For three hours before school, the pair worked their way through the books. Barry's mother sprinkled her lessons liberally with moral advice.

"If you want to grow into a human being, you're going to need some values," she said. When Barry complained about the early morning study sessions she warned him, "This is no picnic for me either, buster."

After a few years, Barry's mother still worried that the extra schoolwork was not enough. She feared that growing up in Indonesia was an increasingly dangerous place for her son. Under Suharto, the government had lapsed into extreme corruption. Even the smallest interaction with a policeman required a bribe. Every commodity that came in or out of the country went through companies controlled by the president's family or ruling members of the government. Fortunately,

A 1969 picture of Obama (circled) and his classmates at the Besuki school in Indonesia *(Courtesy of AP Images/SDN Menteng 1, HO)*

In this photo, a young Obama sits with his mother, Ann, his stepfather, Lolo Soetoro, and his half-sister, Maya Soetoro. *(Courtesy of Polaris Images)*

money did go toward improving schools and roads. Over the next thirty years the country's average wage would increase from fifty dollars a year to six hundred dollars a year.

Barry saw some of this prosperity. His stepfather got a better job with an American oil company. They moved to a bigger house, with a refrigerator and television. Barry also now had a new baby sister named Maya Kassandra Soetoro.

Still, for Barry's mother the dangers came to a head one evening. Coming home late, Barry was greeted by a neighborhood search party his mother had organized to find him. He had hitchhiked to a friend's farm and discovered an irresistible mud slide. While sliding, Barry cut his arm on barbed wire and wrapped a sock around the cut. When his mother saw the wound, she convinced their only neighbor with a car to drive them to the hospital, despite Soetoro's suggestion they wait until morning. When she and Barry arrived at the hospital, they met the doctors—two young men in boxer shorts playing dominoes. Barry and his mother waited while they finished their game and put on pants. They gave Barry twenty stitches and left him with a large scar.

Fueled by this experience and her increasing marital problems with Soetoro, who drank frequently and had a reputation as a womanizer, Barry's mother decided to take her two children back to the United States, where they would have more opportunities and could grow up in a safer environment. In 1971, she sent Barry home to Gramps and Toot in Honolulu, where he would attend a private school. She and Maya would follow shortly, within a year, she promised, and hopefully by Christmas. She reminded Barry of the fun he'd had with his grandparents the summer before in Hawaii. There had been ice cream, cartoons, and trips to the beach. To sweeten the deal his mother added that he wouldn't have to study at four o'clock in the morning anymore. Soon Barry was on a plane headed away from his home in Indonesia.

Ten years later, Barry would see his stepfather one last time when his mother helped Soetoro travel to Los Angeles. He was treated for liver problems that caused his death when he was fifty-three years old. Over the next twenty years Barry's mother would travel back to Indonesia for six to twelve months at a time. She became a specialist in women's issues and helped village women set up their own businesses and bring their produce to markets.

But this was in the future. Now ten-year-old Barry traveled by himself back to Hawaii, away from his mother and sister. His four years of adventure in Indonesia had come to an end. It would be a memory he would store away that gave him insight into both the differences and the similarities between people. For now, he was on to a new adventure. But questions were beginning to nag at him about his father in Kenya.

two
From Barry to Barack

*I*n the summer of 1971, Barry Obama returned to Honolulu. His grandparents greeted him as he came off the plane, tossing leis made of candy and chewing gum around his neck. Barry held a wooden Indonesian mask, a gift from the copilot, up to his face. Gramps joked that the mask was an improvement and threw an arm over his grandson's shoulder. The three chatted about the welcome home dinner Gramps and Toot had planned, Barry's trip, and everyone in Djarkta. The conversation slowed, and Barry realized that visiting his grandparents was one thing, living with them permanently was another.

His grandparents had changed in his absence. They lived a quieter social life than before. Gramps sold insurance, and his sales calls typically weren't successful, making him irritable. Toot had become the first female vice president of a nearby bank. They lived in a two-bedroom apartment within walking distance to Barry's new school.

As the summer wore on, Barry became restless to start school. He mainly wanted friends. For his grandparents though, Barry's entrance into Punahou Academy was a grand event. After several interviews, the school's admission officer grilled him on his career goals, and sent him on a campus tour with Gramps. The campus's lush, manicured lawns, gleaming white buildings, and colorful flowering trees impressed his grandfather.

"This isn't a school," Gramps whispered to Barry. "This is heaven. You might just get me to go back to school with you."

Punahou Academy's campus occupied seventy-six acres. Founded by Christian missionaries in 1841, the school was one of the largest and most respected private schools in the nation. Students from kindergarten through twelfth grade attended, representing a variety of cultures, customs, and religious beliefs. At the heart of the campus stood the chapel, built over the spring-fed lily pond that was the school's namesake. According to legend, an aging Hawaiian couple who had to travel far for water had prayed for a spring. In a dream, they were told to uproot the stump of an old Hala tree. There they found a clear, sweet spring. They named it *Ka Punahou*, meaning the "New Spring."

When Barry was admitted to Punahou, the school sent home a thick admissions packet. Gramps and Toot pored over the information, learning about the extracurricular activities and the courses that would prepare Barry for college. As they read, they grew more and more excited about this wonderful opportunity for their grandson.

It was with this excitement that Barry entered fifth grade in the fall of 1971. He was one of two black students in his grade. The Indonesian sandals he wore, along with the outdated clothes chosen by his grandfather, added to his feeling of being out of place.

The first day was a ten year old's nightmare. His teacher, Miss Hefty, read his full name, Barack Obama, out loud. His unusual name produced giggles from his classmates. When he asked to be called Barry, his teacher commented that Barack was a beautiful name. Gramps had informed her Barry's father was from Kenya. Adding to his embarrassment, Miss Hefty questioned Barry about his father's tribe. The class only snickered more. One boy asked if Barry's father was a cannibal. A red-haired girl asked if she could touch Barry's hair, it being different from her own.

The kids in his grade had little interest in Barry, who couldn't ride a skateboard or play football. Instead, Barry knew the games he and his stepfather had played—chess, badminton, and soccer. After a few rocky months, he had made a few friends and learned to throw a wobbly football pass. He soon settled in to life at school and to life with his grandparents. After Barry finished his homework, the three of them ate dinner together around the television. In the evening, he and Gramps shared the latest snack foods Gramps had discovered. Barry fell asleep listening to the radio; and although he had found a comfortable niche, his curiosity prompted him to ask questions.

One particular question ate away at him. He wondered about his father. Old photos and family stories provided snippets of information about a father Barry didn't remember. His mother told him he'd inherited his father's brains. Gramps and Toot spoke about his father's brilliance and commitment to bettering the world. They talked about his father being noble and wise.

"It's a fact Bar," Gramps said. "Your dad could handle any situation, and that made everybody like him." Even still, despite his mother's and grandparent's stories and love, Barry felt an empty hole in his life.

In December of 1971, Barry received exciting news. His mother and Maya were coming home. Two weeks later his father would be visiting from Kenya. In the years after their

Obama's father, Barack Obama *(Courtesy of Polaris Images)*

divorce, Barry's parents had corresponded through letters, although both had remarried. Obama and his next wife Ruth had three sons, David, Bernard, and Abo, before they divorced. Barry now had four half brothers and two half sisters.

After Barry's mother arrived, she started filling Barry with information about Kenya and its history. Barry embellished these facts to his friends at school, telling them that his father was an African prince. Barry said that he could go to Africa and be a prince if he wanted, adding that the name Obama really meant "Burning Spear."

After ten mysterious years of waiting, Barry wasn't sure what his father would be like. He had no memories of him. As the day of his father's arrival neared, Barry grew more apprehensive. Finally, when he met his father for the first time he could remember, Barry was unsure of what to say or do. Obama was tall and thin, with yellow-tinged eyes, showing that he'd had malaria more than once. He pulled three wooden figurines out of his travel bag—an elephant, a lion, and a man beating a drum, and handed them to Barry, who shyly muttered his thanks.

Barry's father stayed with them for a month, filling the rooms with his deep confident voice, his big laugh, and his love of music. He informed Barry that he expected big things of him. However, tension built as Barry's father began to give orders. Matters came to a head one night over the Christmas cartoon *How the Grinch Stole Christmas*. Barry's father commanded him to turn off the television and go study in his room. Ann jumped in to say that the cartoon was a Christmas favorite.

"He has been watching that machine constantly, and now it is time for him to study," Obama said. His father suggested that Barry didn't work as hard as he should, and that he could begin on the next day's work.

"Go now, before I get angry at you," he told Barry.

Barry went to his room and slammed the door. Afterwards, he listened to the adults outside arguing about who should set the rules. Eventually, Toot came in after Obama left and told Barry he could watch the last five minutes of the television show. Obama's arrival had turned Barry's life upside down. Barry began to count down the days until his father left and life would go back to normal.

Then his father unexpectedly smoothed Barry's path in school. Miss Hefty had invited Barry's father to speak in her classroom—one of the worst possible events Barry could imagine. He worried that the talk would expose his exaggerations and lies about his father. Afterwards, he would have to endure jokes about mud huts and loin cloths. Instead, Obama spoke vividly about Kenya, painting colorful images of its people and history. Barry and the other students were enthralled. After listening to Barry's father, the kids warmed to their new classmate, agreeing that his father was cool.

Barry's feelings toward his father slowly warmed. Together, they read books and went to a University of Hawaii basketball game. His father gave him a basketball for Christmas, sparking basketball fever in the ten-year-old. On his last day in Hawaii, Obama gave his son two records of African music and showed him an African dance, a small window into Barry's paternal heritage. His father had wanted Ann, Barry, and Maya to come back to Kenya with him, but the three of them remained in Hawaii when he left. He and Barry would exchange letters over the years, but would never see each other again.

Obama sits with some of his classmates at the Punahou Academy. *(Courtesy of Punahou School Archives)*

Barry attended Punahou Academy for the next seven years, combining his B+ average with a bit of a mischievous streak. He dribbled his basketball to class and down the school's hallways. When others hid in the cafeteria's shade on hot days, Barry shot hoops on the school's basketball court, as the asphalt steamed in the sun.

Shortly after Barry's father returned to Kenya, Barry's small family moved into a tiny apartment one block from Punahou. His mother was working on a graduate degree in anthropology at the University of Hawaii. Although she received grant money for her studies, time was short, and money was tight. Barry watched Maya, grocery shopped, did laundry, and took a job scooping ice cream. Sometimes Barry's life seemed like a jumbled up puzzle. "I had to reconcile a lot of different threads growing up—race, class," he wrote years later. "For example, I was going to a fancy prep school, and my mother was on food stamps while she was getting her Ph.D."

His mother planned to return to Indonesia for fieldwork. Barry chose to stay behind with his grandparents, continuing with the life he knew, rather than facing more change. It was a difficult decision for everyone. However, Maya thought one reason Barry didn't want to leave Hawaii was because of his rising popularity. "He had powers," she said. "He was charismatic. He had lots of friends."

At Punahou, Barry began to write for the school's literary journal, *Ka Wai Ola,* which meant "The Living Water." He also threw himself into basketball. In his last two years at school, he neared six feet two inches in height and made the school's basketball team. He was the team's only left-hander and played forward. Punahou's team was excellent. Because of his talent for nailing long jump shots, Barry's teammates nicknamed him "Barry O'Bomber." The Punahou team placed second in the state championships Barry's first year. The following year, they won first place. His coach Chris McLachlin admired how much Barry loved the game.

Obama puts up a shot in this 1979 photo. *(Courtesy of Punahou School Archives)*

"He loved the game so much that he'd do anything to practice," McLachlin said. "He snuck past teachers when they opened the gym's locked doors. When no one was around, he broke into the gym."

But family, strong education, and a love a basketball weren't enough to keep Barry out of trouble. He didn't fit neatly into any one group, and racial pressures threatened to overwhelm him at times. "I learned to slip back and forth between my black and white worlds convinced that with a bit of translation on my part the two worlds would eventually cohere," he wrote years later.

Barry and other black students at Punahou Academy shared their anger over racism. Barry recalled a bad joke about his color rubbing off on a tennis tournament schedule if he touched it, and a woman's fearful looks when he stepped onto an elevator with her. He struggled with racial divisions and prejudices. Then one day it came from an unexpected direction. That morning, when Toot waited for the bus, a man persistently pestered her for money. When Barry heard the story, Gramps told him his grandmother was afraid because the man was black. It was like a punch in the stomach.

"Never had they given me reason to doubt their love," Barry said of his grandparents. "I doubted if they ever would. And yet I knew that men who might easily have been my brothers could still inspire their rawest fears."

Barry's grades at school began to slip. He stopped writing to his father. His mother, back from her fieldwork, confronted him about his grades. She also wanted to know the details of his friend who was arrested for possessing drugs. Barry himself had begun to experiment with drugs, trying both marijuana and cocaine. Neither his mother, nor his school, knew what to do with him. The root of the problem was that Barry didn't know what to do with himself. "Junkie, pothead," Barry wrote later. "That's where I'd been headed: the final, fatal role of the young, would-be black man."

Fortunately, Barry turned in a different direction and found a new way to defuse his anger and confusion. He read incessantly. In his struggle to accept himself, and abate his loneliness, he looked to famous authors, particularly men who had learned how to deal with being black in a white-powered country. Barry read works by poet Langston Hughes

In order to diffuse his frustration with racism and feelings of alienation, Obama turned to the writings of famous black authors such as Langston Hughes. *(Library of Congress)*

W. E. B. Du Bois *(Library of Congress)*

and writers Ralph Ellison and Richard Wright and studied such activists as W. E. B. Du Bois, one of the founders of the National Association for the Advancement of Colored People (NAACP). Barry read to discover meaning in his life. He developed new heroes—Martin Luther King, Jr., Mahatma Gandhi, and Cesar Chavez, all men who accomplished great things through peaceful means.

Finally, on a better path, Barry graduated from Punahou Academy without mishap. Several colleges accepted him, but he wasn't especially interested in any of them. The summer before, he had met a girl from Occidental College, near Pasadena,

Dr. Martin Luther King Jr. became a hero to Obama. *(Library of Congress)*

California. The school, located near Los Angeles, was as good a place as any to attend. Two thousand students attended the California hillside campus. They walked past palm trees on their way to classes in white buildings with red-tiled roofs.

Barry began his life at Occidental once again struggling to find his place. He found a group of friends set on making their resistance to racial discrimination public. Barry wanted to establish his credentials as a black man. At one point, he made fun of another friend, a black, middle-class student, who dressed well and had a white girlfriend. Barry's dorm mate advised him to spend more time ensuring that his own life was together, and less passing judgment on other's acts. The incident shamed Barry and he came to see it as a reflection of his own fear of not belonging. He realized that both the white world of his mother and the black world of his father were a part of him. It was a defining moment in his life, accepting both of his heritages. Barry claimed his voice and identity. He decided to drop his nickname and go by his Kenyan name, Barack. "Only a lack of imagination, a failure of nerve had made me think that I had to choose" between them—his two racial identities—he said later.

Barack's stint at Occidental provided him with other important lessons. It was here that he received his first taste of political action. At the time, many of the students on campus were speaking out against the mistreatment of black people in South Africa, where the government's racist practices appalled the international world. Barack joined students at Occidental who were calling for colleges to stop conducting business with South Africa's government.

One afternoon, Barack spoke in public on a political issue for the first time. Students tossing Frisbees on the campus lawn stopped to listen. In a staged protest, two white students dragged Barack off stage. The idea was to symbolize the silencing of the black voice. Barack had seen and heard that words have the power to change minds.

After two years at Occidental College, Barack needed a change. He was eager to escape the sprawl of Los Angeles. In the fall of 1981, he took advantage of an exchange program between Occidental and Columbia University in New York City.

He thrived on the energy of New York City—from the honking horns to the fast-paced crowds, and twenty-four-hours-a-day action. Barack studied hard, ran three miles a day, and fasted on Sundays. He also began to grasp even more deeply the divisions between race and class in America's society.

A year after Barack arrived at Columbia he received sad news from his Aunt Jane in Nairobi. His father had died in a car accident. He was forty-six years old. Although Barack had hardly known his father, he began to dream about him.

He realized that one day he would need to go to Kenya to learn more about his father.

Barack graduated from college two years later, in 1983, with a degree in political science. He had pressing concerns, such as the need to find a job and earn some money. He had to delay his dream of traveling to Kenya to uncover his roots.

three
A Crumbling Community

After Barack Obama graduated from Columbia University, he searched for a job as a community organizer. He wanted to promote civil rights in decaying neighborhoods like those he had observed in New York City. Unable to find such work, he took a job as a research assistant for Business International Corporation. The job had the benefit of paying more than a community organizer's salary, and he had college loans to pay off. He quickly moved from research assistant to financial writer, receiving higher pay.

Obama considered staying with the company. The pay was good and he had the opportunity for advancement. Then something happened to make him change his mind. He had been writing to his half sister, Auma, and the two had been planning to visit each other, but neither of them had enough money, and the plans were vague. Now Auma was planning a trip to the United States with some friends, and asked if she could visit him in New York. Obama spent the next few weeks sprucing up his apartment. But two days before her arrival, she called to tell Obama that their young half brother David had been killed in a motorcycle accident. She needed to return to Kenya instead.

Obama tried to comfort Auma, but he also wondered about what unfulfilled dreams David might have had. It again sparked his dream of finding a job helping communities in need. He wanted to be a part of something bigger than himself, bigger than just setting his sights on more money and an office with a better view. "There's nothing wrong with making money, but focusing your life solely on making a buck shows a poverty of ambition," Obama said later.

After graduating from Columbia University, Obama moved to Chicago to pursue a career in community organization.

In 1983, Obama sent out more applications for community organizing jobs. Six months later, Jerry Kellman offered him a job in Chicago, Illinois. Kellman later became the character "Marty" in a book Obama would write. For $10,000 a year, Obama would work for the Developing Communities Project in Chicago's South Side. The area housed some of the city's poorest neighborhoods. Many of these communities had been hit hard when local plants closed and laid off employees. Now families were fighting merely to eat and keep their electricity on. Obama hoped to improve their run-down living conditions by organizing the residents.

Years later he would write, "It was in these neighborhoods that I received the best education I ever had."

Obama felt at home in Chicago. In his car, he traced the shoreline of Lake Michigan, and found the theater where Duke Ellington and Ella Fitzgerald performed. He also recalled reading about black author Richard Wright's days of delivering mail in Chicago while he waited for his first book to be published. On Obama's third day, he wandered into a neighborhood that radiated a sense of warmth and friendliness. He found a barbershop owned by a man called Smitty. More than twenty years later, Obama would still get his hair cut at Smitty's.

Obama was assigned to work with the Altgeld Gardens Public Housing Project, on the city's southernmost edge. Altgeld contained 2,000 apartments in a series of two-story brick buildings with army green doors and grimy, fake shutters. Its crumbling ceilings and backed-up toilets were infamous among residents. Muddy tire tracks created ruts in the small, brown lawns; no gardens were to be found in Altgeld Gardens.

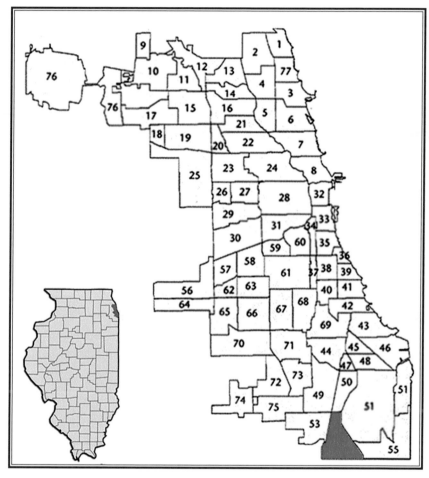

Altgeld Gardens was located in southern Chicago.

Obama slowly made contacts. He worked with Yvonne Lloyd, mother of eleven children. (Lloyd became the basis for the character "Shirley," in Obama's book *Dreams from My Father.* When writing the book, Obama altered the names of some of the characters to maintain their privacy. He also created composite characters to give readers the flavor of the people with whom he worked.) Some of the community organizers banded together to help each other, as many

Altgeld Gardens, the housing projects where Obama worked to address issues of poverty, discrimination, and health concerns *(Photo courtesy of AP Images/Charles Rex Arbogast)*

of them faced similar issues with the project housing they hoped to improve.

Obama was young and enthusiastic, but the job he had embarked on seemed thankless at times. Many of the people he met scraped by for money and food and didn't have time to tackle bigger social issues. He went to local churches, hoping to garner support.

"He went from church to church, beating the pavement, trying to get every pastor in the community," recalled

Reverend Alvin Love. "This skinny, scrawny guy trying to find out how we can make the community better. He just walked the streets."

Obama called meetings with the local residents. At first, few people showed up, not even the church leaders. He polled residents on their problems, listening to their issues and hearing echoes of his grandparents' and mother's stories about the drive for something more in life. He focused on these stories. Obama also noted that, "people carried within them some central explanation of themselves. Stories full of terror and wonder, studded with events that still haunted or inspired them. Sacred stories." The stories he heard matched his own at times, helping to give him a sense of community and bind his world together. "There was poetry there as well—a luminous world always present beneath the surface, a world that people might offer up as a gift to me, if I only remembered to ask."

Soon Obama had another piece to his own story. His half sister, Auma came to visit. She was living in Heidelberg, Germany finishing up a master's degree in linguistics. At the airport, they met after many years, hugging and laughing together, and instantly making a family connection. Later they shared stories about their work. Auma talked about the difficulties of living in Germany and dealing with German prejudices.

"If you scratch the surface you see they still have the attitudes of their childhood," she said. "In German fairy tales, black people are always the goblins. Such things one doesn't forget so easily."

Over a cup of tea, Auma also told Obama about their father, whom she called the Old Man. "I can't say I really knew him, Barack," she started. "Maybe nobody did . . . not really. His life was so scattered. People only knew scraps and pieces, even his own children."

Auma continued to recount the tale, beginning when their father returned to Kenya with his American wife, Ruth. Auma and her brother Roy went to live with their father. The Old Man worked for an American oil company and became wealthy and connected with top government people. His big car, big house, American wife, and education impressed everyone. During this time, he had two sons, Mark and David, with Ruth, and two sons, Abo and Bernard, with Auma's mother, Kezia.

Divisions in Kenya began to affect the family though, especially when their father started working for the government. President Jomo Kenyatta was from the largest tribe in Africa, the Kikuyus. Under him, the government became increasingly corrupt. The Luos began to protest that the Kikuyus were getting all the top jobs. People were killed in police crackdowns. When the Old Man spoke up, he lost his job. Through the strong arms of the president, he was denied work everywhere, even outside the country. He began to drink heavily, and when Auma was about twelve years old, Ruth left with her two sons. Their father had a serious car accident, killing a farmer, and spending a year in the hospital recuperating.

For a while, the Obamas had no place to live, shamefully having to borrow money for food. Auma resented her father for still putting on airs. She said he often talked about Barry and Ann in the United States, sharing their letters as if to show that someone had cared for him once.

Eventually, Roy left, and Auma began to attend Kenya High School on scholarship, which helped mold her life. Gradually,

After Jomo Kenyatta became president of Kenya, the government became corrupt and Obama's father lost his government position. *(Courtesy of AP Images)*

the family's situation improved. President Kenyatta died and the Old Man got a government job again. Auma left for Germany, seeing her father one last time at an international conference. By then the Old Man had one more son, George, while living with a young woman. Auma began to cry as she reached the end of her story. "I was just starting to know him," she sobbed. " . . . when he died, I felt so . . . so cheated. As cheated as you must have felt."

For Obama the story came as a shock, shattering his image a father who had remained fixed in his mind as he was years before when he visited Hawaii. Yet, for all this new information, he still didn't know his father and his ambitions.

Fifteen days later, before Auma left she said it best. "We need to go home," she said. "We need to go home, Barack, and see him there."

She was right, but for now Obama still had his work in Chicago driving him. He needed to continue what he had started. Kenya had to wait for another day.

With Obama helping to organize local residents, support slowly grew for more projects to improve their lives, such as neighborhood cleanups. With help, he instituted crime watch programs, lobbied to improve sanitation services, and brought job training programs to the neighborhoods.

Obama focused on local schools as well. He met with Dr. Martha Collier, an elementary school principal in Altgeld. In the hallway, she and Obama stopped to watch a line of five- and six-year-olds enter a classroom. Despite their difficult home environments, they were happy, curious, and trusting. "The change comes later," Collier commented. ". . . their eyes stop laughing. Their throats can still make the sound, but if you look at their eyes, you can see they've shut off something inside."

Collier arranged for Obama to meet with the children's parents, many of them in their late teens or early twenties. He spent several hours each week talking to both the children and their families. He had them canvass the blocks with complaint forms, getting residents to identify local problems.

One day, someone showed Obama a newspaper clipping, and he realized he had found an issue the neighborhood could tackle. It was an ad from the Chicago Housing Authority soliciting for contractors to remove asbestos from Altgeld's management office. Asbestos, an insulator and fire-retardant, can be still be found in older homes. It was used in pipe and

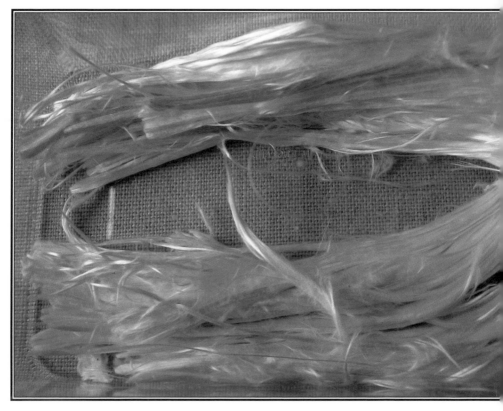

When released into the air, asbestos fibers can cause many health threats, including cancer.

furnace insulation, shingles, textured paints, and floor tiles. If cut or disturbed, however, asbestos fibers can be released into the air, accumulating in people's lungs. While there are no immediate symptoms, there is a long-term risk of abdominal and lung cancer and other lung diseases. In 1989, the Environmental Protection Agency succeeded in banning virtually all products containing asbestos, following many years of debate.

After seeing the housing authority's ad, Obama questioned Altgeld's residents to determine if any of them had been notified about their potential exposure to asbestos. They had not.

He and a resident set up an appointment to talk to the manager of Altgeld's office. Although he hoped other residents would show up, they did not. The manager assured Obama and the resident that asbestos testing had been done in the apartments and promised to show them a copy of the tests within a week. After a week, the test results had not shown up. Calls and letters to the office went unreturned.

The group drafted a letter to the downtown Chicago Housing Authority office, saying they would appear there in two days for an answer to their questions. To encourage residents to join the group going downtown by school bus, people called their neighbors and teachers sent letters home from school pinned to children's jackets. Obama also issued a press release.

The day of the trip, only eight people, beyond the organizers, showed up for the protest. One of them dubbed the small group "Obama's Army."

When the "army" arrived at the Housing Authority's office, they asked to see the director. The receptionist told them that wasn't possible and suggested she might call security if they did not leave. At that moment, the media showed up, starting a press conference about the asbestos testing. As soon as cameras began rolling, a woman quickly ushered the residents into an office. Once in the meeting, the residents discovered no testing had been done. They extracted a promise that testing would begin by day's end. They also got a meeting with the director. The protest was a success.

"I changed as a result of that bus trip," Obama wrote later. "That bus ride kept me going, I think. Maybe it still does."

Obama continued his work with local schools. He met with Asante Moran, a high school counselor in Altgeld. He hoped to provide mentoring and tutoring for male teenagers, while involving parents. Moran asked Obama about his name, questioning when he last traveled back to Africa. Obama surprised Moran by saying he'd never gone.

"The people were so welcoming," Moran said. "And the land—I'd never seen anything so beautiful. It really felt like I had come home." He told Obama that the trip would change his life.

Obama continued his work as a community organizer, but his thoughts were elsewhere. Kenya tugged at him. He decided to meet his half brother Roy, who lived in Washington, D.C. After attending the University of Nairobi, Roy had married an American Peace Corps worker and moved to the United States. When Obama stepped off the plane to meet Roy, he wasn't there. When he called his half brother, Roy suggested that Obama find a hotel room instead, as he and his wife were having marital problems. They agreed to meet for dinner.

Over dinner, Obama heard more tales about the Old Man. Roy bitterly explained the high expectations their father had set. As the eldest son, after his father's death, all family duties fell to Roy. His responsibilities included ensuring good marriages, providing housing, paying schooling fees, and more, including making his father's funeral arrangements.

"People came . . . from everywhere, and we had to mourn him according to Luo tradition, burning a log for three days, listening to people cry and moan," Roy explained. "Half these people, I didn't even know who they were. They wanted food. They wanted beer. Some whispered that the Old Man had been poisoned, that I must take revenge. Some people stole things from the house. Then our relatives began to fight about the Old Man's inheritance."

Roy continued until he reached the point of David's death. David's mother had tried to raise him to ignore his African heritage. He rebelled, running away from home, and staying with Roy. David's death convinced Roy that the family was cursed. He left Kenya to start over.

Although Obama suggested they share the heavy load, it made little difference to Roy. Discouraged, and without money to pay for another night at a hotel, Obama flew home the next day. His visit with Roy had only provided a glimpse at unknown relatives.

Not only was Obama facing nagging family questions, but he was getting frustrated by the snail's pace of his work as an organizer. Three years after he arrived in Chicago, Obama decided to make a change. He decided to go to law school. He applied to Harvard, Yale, and Stanford.

Obama worried that people would think he was deserting them. "Ain't nobody gonna get the wrong idea, Barack," his fellow organizer Johnnie said. "Man, we're just proud to see you succeed."

Obama vowed that he would learn about the legislative process, along with business and legal practices, so that he could bring his knowledge back to the people, and incite real change. He had decided that many of the community's problems were caused by the skewed priorities of the politicians in local and national government. While Obama waited to hear whether he was accepted, he continued his work.

Obama began to focus on local churches. He met Reverend Jeremiah Wright Jr., the pastor of Trinity United Church of Christ. Wright's church had a commitment to the black community, to promote education, work, discipline, and self respect. He appealed to younger people, and his church served

Obama speaks at the Trinity United Church of Christ. *(Courtesy of AP Images/Nam Y. Huh)*

as a model for what other ministers hoped to accomplish. The silver-haired reverend had grown up in Philadelphia, as the son of a Baptist minister. Wright had joined the Marines, dabbled with Islam, Black Nationalism, and liquor, before ending up at the University of Chicago for graduate work. After six years, he received his PhD in the history of religion, learning both Hebrew and Greek. Wright's diversity and understanding helped him hold his church together. It had grown from two hundred to 4,000 members.

"We've got a lot of different personalities here," Wright told Obama. "Got the Africanist over here. The traditionalist over here. Once in a while I have to stick my hand in the pot—smooth things over before stuff gets ugly. But that's rare. Usually, if somebody's got an idea for a new ministry, I just tell 'em to run with it and get outta their way."

Something in Wright's words swayed Obama. One Sunday he woke, shaved, dressed in his only suit, and arrived at the church by seven-thirty in the morning. The church quickly filled with women wearing wide-plumed hats and men in suits and ties. Other men wore mud-cloth kufis, or short, rounded hats dyed by using traditional African methods.

The day's sermon was titled "The Audacity of Hope." Reverend Wright told about the painting of a harpist sitting atop a mountain with only one string left on her instrument. She was tattered and worn, everything below her stood in ruins, but still she dared to hope, sending her music to the heavens on one string. Wright compared the woman's struggles to those of his congregation, the hardships, the pains, the scraping money together to pay the bills.

The power of Wright's message struck a deep chord within Obama. It would stay with him for years, turning over in his head, inspiring him again and again. That day sparked his own faith. He realized that the center of a community was grounded in many elements—political, economical, social, and spiritual. Faith was more than just a comfort for the weary; it was also an active agent in the world and could spur social change.

After meeting Reverend Wright, Obama forged ahead with his life. Accepted by several law schools, he settled on Harvard, like his father. But before starting school in the fall, he decided to face some of the questions that had plagued him for his entire life. He needed to explore his African roots. He planned a trip to Kenya to fill in the blanks of his family history.

four

Spirits of the Past

I n 1987, twenty-six-year-old Barack Obama began his quest to understand his father. He planned to spend a few weeks traveling in Europe, before a monthlong visit with family in Kenya. Armed with a guidebook, Obama traveled alone by bus and train through Europe. He drank tea by the Thames River in London. He watched children chase each other, threading through the trees, in the famed Luxembourg Gardens in Paris. As his time in Kenya drew closer, he found himself becoming increasingly edgy and hesitant. The Old Man's ghost was waiting for him.

As Obama's plane touched down at Kenyatta International Airport, behind was the backdrop of an African dawn— rounded hills against a sky streaked with high thin clouds tinged red. Despite the dramatic entrance, he soon realized his luggage was lost. A woman helping him with some forms asked if was related to Dr. Obama. When he explained Dr. Obama was his father, she struck up a conversation. For

Obama visited the famous Luxembourg Gardens while traveling through Europe.

Obama this was something new. In the United States, no one had ever connected his name with his father's. Here he already had an identity—and it was a new and comforting feeling.

Soon Obama was in the arms of Auma and Auntie Zeituni, his father's sister. "Welcome home," said Zeituni, kissing him on both cheeks.

The three climbed into Auma's car excitedly talking about Obama's visit, the people he would meet, and the plans they had made. Grassy plains stretched out on either side of the road. Gradually, the traffic thickened as more people started out for work. Obama saw bicycles, cars, and *matatus,* rickety public minibuses. Along with other pedestrians walked straight-backed women, their heads wrapped in colorful

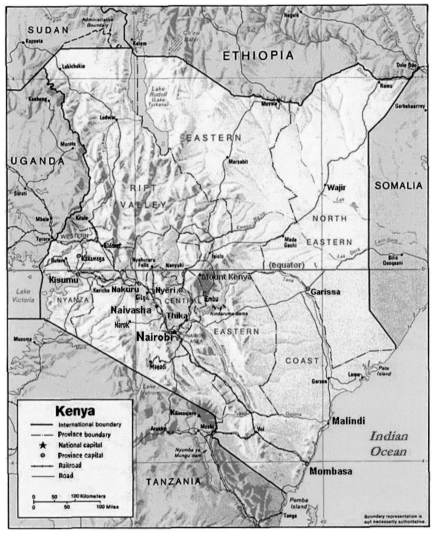

Map of Kenya

scarves. When they stopped to drop Zeituni off at work she leaned over to kiss Obama again. "You take good care of Barry now," she said to Auma. "Make sure he doesn't get lost again."

Obama asked Auma what their aunt meant about getting lost. Auma explained it was a common expression used after not seeing someone for a while. She also explained that it had a more serious meaning at times. Sometimes, a son or husband moved to the West, promising to return. At first they wrote once a week, then once a month, then they stopped, and were never seen again. "They've been lost, you see," said Auma. "Even if people know where they are."

That evening, Auma took Obama to meet relatives in Kariako, east of Nairobi. They entered Aunt Jane's apartment, and she hugged Obama. A crowd of people smiled behind her. Jane introduced Obama to Kezia, the Old Man's first wife.

"My son," Kezia said in Swahili. "My son has come home."

Aunts, cousins, nephews, and nieces passed Obama around the room. Together, the family ate goat curry, fried fish, collard greens, and rice, as they peppered each other with friendly questions. When Obama and Auma left, Jane suggested they visit Sarah, the Old Man's older sister next.

Auma explained to Obama in the car that there were some hard feelings in his newfound family. Sarah disputed the Old Man's will, fearing all of his inheritance would go to his wives, instead of to her. Their visit to Sarah at the end of the week was filled with tension, as she focused on family lies and her own lack of money. Obama was seeing another side of the coin, the one that had worried Roy as the family caretaker. Already, family in Kenya looked to Obama for money and support.

But Obama was also experiencing a circle of family unlike any he had ever known before. People greeted Dr. Obama's long-lost son in stores, at parks, and on the street. Relatives showered him with invitations. But he saw that life in Nairobi was difficult. His family, like many others, sometimes had trouble putting food on the table, and had to reserve doctor's visits for emergencies.

One night, he and Auma shared their thoughts on the subject, both worrying that they owed more to their family in Kenya.

"Sometimes I have this dream that I will build a beautiful house on our grandfather's land," Auma began. "A big house where we can all stay and bring our families, you see. We could plant fruit trees like our grandfather, and our children would really know the land and speak Luo and learn our ways from the old people. It would belong to them."

But for Auma, the dream ended there. She worried her family would come to depend on her for everything. She wasn't ready for that responsibility.

Auntie Zeituni put it into perspective for Obama. She told him of the times when the Old Man was out of favor with the government. People were afraid to be seen with him, for fear of retribution. They forgot him, laughed at him. Even family refused to take him in, telling him it was too dangerous. Afterwards though, he never held a grudge, helping the same people who had betrayed him. Zeituni explained the pressures Obama's father faced in Kenya.

"You must learn from his life. If you have something, then everyone will want a piece of it. So you have to draw the line somewhere," Zeituni said. "If everyone is family, no one is family. Your father, he never understood this, I think."

Obama mulled his aunt's words. He also began to explore Nairobi. In the old marketplace, peddlers hawked bright brass jewelry, wooden trinkets, ripe fruit, colorful fabrics, and woven baskets. He saw Masai women, carrying their goods on their heads, their slender bodies in bright red *shukas*, or wraps, their earlobes elongated with beaded earrings, and their clean shaved heads covered in bright head cloths.

During his time in Kenya, Obama was able to explore Nairobi and see members of the native Masai people. *(Courtesy of AP Images/SAYYID AZIM)*

Toward the end of his second week in Kenya, Obama convinced Auma to go on a safari with him. For Obama, the safari showed him a new world. At dawn, he awoke to the silhouettes of black trees against a deep blue sky that filled with orange and creamy yellows as the sun rose high.

"A pride of lions, yawning in the broken grass," he wrote later of his sights. "Buffalo in the marshes, their horns like cheap wigs . . . Hippos in the shallow riverbeds, pink eyes and nostrils like marbles bobbing on water's surface."

The beauty and stillness awed Obama. He and Auma returned to Nairobi, finding that Roy had arrived. After the quiet of the African plains, the excitement of his family at Roy's homecoming dinner surrounded Obama. Soon they all made plans to travel to rural western Kenya. It was one leg in their long journey home to Alego, the lands of their grandfather. After an all-night train ride, they would take a five-hour *matatu* ride to Home Squared, a term children in Nairobi used.

"There's your ordinary house in Nairobi. And then there's your house in the country, where your people come from," Roy explained. "Your ancestral home. Even the biggest minister or businessman thinks this way. . . . When we were at school and we wanted to tell somebody we were going to Alego, it was home twice over, you see. Home Squared."

They joked that for Obama it would be Home Cubed. On the train, Auma regaled him with tales of Alego and its beauty. As children, she and Roy loved traveling to Alego, visiting Granny, with her wonderful sense of humor, and their grandfather, whom they called the Terror, because of his temper.

The family arrived in Kisumu, crammed into an over-crowded bus with bald tires and few seats. Obama sat for hours on the bus, holding Auma on his lap, along with a stranger's squealing baby, and a basket of yams. Eventually, they arrived in Alego.

Obama's grandfather's compound was one of the biggest in the area. In the middle of it stood a low, rectangular house, with a corrugated iron roof, and concrete walls. Bougainvillea spread on one side of the house, dotting it with colorful pink, yellow, and red flowers. Nearby, a few pecking chickens sur-rounded a small round hut lined with earthenware pots. A wide grassy yard separated two more huts, and underneath a tall mango tree two placid, bony, red cows grazed. Inside the sparsely furnished home, Obama found a few wooden chairs and some family's artifacts on the wall, such as the Old Man's diploma from Harvard.

Obama met his stepgrandmother, Sarah Hussein Onyango, whose sparkling eyes accompanied her big hugs. Both she and Obama attempted to greet each other in the other's lan-guage. Granny laughed and spoke to Auma. "She says she has dreamed about this day, when she would finally meet this son of her son," Auma translated. "She says you've brought her a great happiness. She says that now you have finally come home."

Both Granny and Obama wanted to be able to say more to each other, without having to rely on Auma. Obama asked his half sister to tell her that he'd like to learn Luo, but he was busy in the States.

"She understands that," said Auma, translating Granny's response. "But she also says that a man can never be too busy to know his own people."

A photo of Obama with his stepgrandmother, Sarah Hussein Onyango
(Courtesy of AP Images/Sayyid Azim)

That night as they ate, they heard a strange sound in the distance. Auma joked that the night-runners, or spirit men, were out. Granny had told them stories about the night-runners. In the daytime the night-runners looked like ordinary men. At night though, they took the shape of leopards. They caused problems and stole people's goats and cattle. But their

Obama's ancestral home is close to Lake Victoria, seen here.

grandfather had not been afraid of them. He'd even chased one with his *panga*, or machete, when a night-runner stole their baby goat. Just as he was about to catch it, the night-runner leaped into the trees, dropping the goat.

Obama sat, as family tales wove around him. The next day after walking around the lands, he and his family traveled to Kendu Bay, on the shores of Lake Victoria, to meet more relatives. After several hours in an old jalopy, Obama caught glimpses of Lake Victoria's silvery waters that tapered off into flat, green marshes. He saw women on the riverbanks of a wide chocolate-brown river slapping wet clothes on rocks as goats chewed on yellow grass

Obama's cousin Malik displays a picture taken of Obama (left) in traditional African dress. *(Courtesy of AP Images/Karel Prinsloo)*

nearby. They got out of the car and Obama stood in front of his great-great grandfather's grave—a pile of rocks and sticks. The lands of *K'Obama,* meaning "Land of the Obama," surrounded him. He was one of the *Jok'Obama,* or "the people of Obama." In Kendu Bay, Obama also met his great uncle—the oldest man he'd ever seen. Roy translated the man's words.

"He says that many young men have been lost to . . . the white man's country. He says his own son is in America and has not come home for many years. Such men are like ghosts . . . When they die, no one will be there to mourn them. No ancestors will be there to welcome them. So…it is good that you have returned."

When Obama returned to Home Squared, he met his great aunt, Dorsila, who had walked from her village to meet him. Under the shade of the mango tree that afternoon as high clouds stretched over the hills, Obama found the stories he longed for. Granny spun one story after another, telling Obama about his grandfather, the village herbalist. He had been the first in his clan to trade in his loin cloth for a suit, and learn to speak, write, and read English. Granny told of Obama's father's rebellious teenage years.

After listening to these stories, Obama walked to the two rectangular cement coffins in the compound—his grandfather's and his father's. The plaque on his grandfather's grave indicated his name and that he had died in 1979. Although Obama's father had died six years before, there was no name on his grave. In later years, Roy would place a plaque on the coffin.

Obama sat at his father's grave, thinking about this man he'd hardly known. He had heard tales of his intelligence, his pride, his generosity, and his fallibility. Now Obama wept, as he understood his father, seeing both their differences and their similarities.

"I saw that my life in America—the black life, the white life, the sense of abandonment I'd felt as a boy, the frustration and hope I'd witnessed in Chicago—all of it was connected with this small plot of earth an ocean away, connected by more than the accident of a name or the color of my skin," Obama wrote. "The pain I felt was my father's pain. My questions were my brothers' questions. Their struggle, my birthright."

On a bright day in Home Squared, Obama finally sensed the peace that he had been looking for. He had found a place to set his feet firmly on the ground. It was time now for him to return to the United States. Harvard waited. But he would return to Kenya again one day.

After visiting his ancestral homelands and meeting his paternal relatives, Obama felt at peace with his African heritage. *(Courtesy of AP Images/Gary Knight /VII)*

five

Hope and Ambitions

*I*n the fall of 1988, Obama entered Harvard Law School. He applied himself to his studies, spending hours in the library, poring over cases and laws. He believed that the work he was doing now would one day help others.

"On first impression, he seemed older than he was," remembered Kenneth Mack, Obama's classmate, currently an assistant professor at Harvard. "I thought of him as a black guy with a midwestern accent. But he seemed experienced in the world in ways some of us weren't. He spoke well and concisely in a way that seemed wise and broad-minded."

Because of the stress brought on by his intense studies, Obama turned once again to one of his favorite hobbies to unwind—basketball. To him, the basketball star Michael Jordan symbolized focus and intense competition.

Obama's hard work soon paid off. At the end of his first year he made *Harvard Law Review,* one of the highest honors for a law student. Candidates submit their grades, along

Obama quickly made a name for himself at Harvard Law School, becoming the first African American president of the *Harvard Law Review*. *(Courtesy of AP Images/Chitose Suzuki)*

with a writing sample. Those who are selected write or edit articles for the monthly journal. After one year, all of the editors chose Obama as president of the *Review*. He was the first African American to receive this honor. Obama became the center of much media attention. Law firms eagerly recruited him and a publisher contracted Obama to write his autobiography.

Obama's constitutional law professor, Laurence Tribe, chose him as his research assistant. Later, Tribe called him, "one of the two most talented students I've had in thirty-seven years of teaching."

Obama spent two more years at Harvard Law School. He grew to respect the legal system in many ways, primarily because it represented a promise of justice, even if that justice was not always served. As long as people still asked questions about what was just, there was the hope that what binds people together will triumph over what separates them. Obama described the law as a nation's historical memory. "The law also records a long-running conversation, a nation arguing with its conscience."

The summer before Obama graduated from Harvard Law, he clerked at a large corporate law firm in Chicago, Sidley & Austin. He struggled though, because such a firm was worlds away from the poor neighborhoods he wished to serve. But with his law school bills mounting, he couldn't turn down a good three-month salary. Obama found a cheap apartment and bought three new suits. He also bought a pair of shoes that were about a half size too small. He described them as crippling for the next nine weeks.

That summer, Obama worked for wealthy clients in a sometimes cut-throat atmosphere. In the process he realized corporate law was not for him, and came to appreciate even more how strong his ties were to Chicago, and how much the city felt like home. He also fell in love with Michelle LaVaughn Robinson, a lawyer at the firm.

They met on a drizzly June morning. Robinson was responsible for showing Obama around the office that summer. Although three years younger, Robinson had graduated from Princeton

University and received her law degree from Harvard before Obama. Robinson planned to specialize in entertainment law. Smart, funny, and charming, she had grown up on Chicago's South Side, in a bungalow just north of the neighborhoods where Obama had worked as an organizer. Her father, Fraser, worked as a city pump operator; her mother, Marian, was a housewife and then a secretary at a bank.

For weeks, Obama saw Robinson in the law library, in the cafeteria, and on law firm outings. They soon started dating. When Robinson took Obama home to meet her parents, he was drawn to the warm atmosphere of their home. He quickly hit it off with Robinson's brother Craig—a former basketball star at Princeton. Robinson's family had faced difficulties living in Chicago in the 1950s and 1960s, when divisions between races often led to violence on the streets. Robinson's father also had been diagnosed with multiple sclerosis when he was thirty years old. Multiple Sclerosis is a disease affecting the central nervous system and can cause

Michelle Robinson Obama *(Courtesy of AP Images/Jeff Roberson)*

pain, numbness, difficulty walking, and fatigue. Robinson's family had met these challenges and remained strong. To Obama, her family represented stability and peace. " ... there were uncles and aunts and cousins everywhere, stopping by to sit around the kitchen table and eat until they burst and tell wild stories and listen to Grandpa's old jazz collection and laugh deep into the night," he wrote.

After that summer, Obama returned for his last year at Harvard. He kept Michelle in his heart though, and knew he would return to Chicago to look for a job. In 1991, when he graduated, opulent law firms flung their doors open to him. He was offered jobs at Wall Street firms, as well as a clerkship on the U.S. Court of Appeals, a fast track to clerking on the U.S. Supreme Court. One attorney, Judson Miner, from Miner, Barnhill & Galland, called the *Harvard Law Review* offices to leave his phone number.

Years later Miner remembered a woman answering the phone. "She said 'I'll put you on the list, you're number 643' or something like that," he recalled. Obama was already a hot commodity.

Despite Obama's pick of jobs at prestigious law firms, Miner's Chicago-based firm would be a good match for him because it was a smaller practice focusing on civil rights cases. Obama took the job. At Miner's firm, he could draw on his experience as a community organizer.

During this time, Obama and Robinson became engaged. She met his mother, Toot, and Gramps—and they all approved of the marriage heartily. The pair also traveled to Kenya, where Robinson quickly scored points with his family by picking up more words in Luo than he did. They met more Kenyan relatives and traveled the country, noting both its beauty and how the economy and corruption had worsened. They soon returned to the United States after many happy reunions in Home Squared.

Shortly before their marriage, Robinson's father passed away. He died soon after a kidney operation, never having the chance to walk his daughter down the aisle. Gramps died a few months later, after a long battle with prostate cancer. A World War II veteran, he was buried at Punchbowl National Cemetery on a hill overlooking Honolulu.

Despite these sorrows, Obama and Robinson decided to go ahead with their wedding. They were married on October 18, 1992, by Reverend Wright at Trinity United Church of Christ in Chicago, surrounded by aunts, uncles, brothers, sisters, their mothers, and their friends. Obama's brother, Roy, now called Abongo for his Luo name, had embraced his African heritage.

For Obama, Abongo acted as the dignified and strong older brother that day, helping to calm his jitters. Obama watched as Maya and Auma danced with Robinson's five- and six-year-old cousins, fitted in kente cloth caps and looking like young African princes. It was a day of pride and joy in both their heritage and the wonderful mix of people around them. They toasted to those who were not there with them, and to happy endings, dribbling their drinks on the floor, a drink to the ancestors, as was a Luo custom.

After Obama and Robinson were married they moved to Hyde Park, a mixed-race neighborhood on Chicago's South Side. Obama began work at the law firm. He helped organizations trying to build grocery stores, housing, and health clinics in the inner city. At times, he represented victims who were embarrassed and angry at the discrimination they

Wedding photo of Obama and his wife Michelle standing beside their mothers *(Courtesy of Polaris Images)*

faced. He wrote briefs and drew up contracts and legal papers. Obama also met many people in local and state politics. It was important fulfilling work, the type he had gone to law school to do in the first place.

Soon Obama added more to his plate. He worked for Illinois Project Vote, an initiative that registered 150,000 voters from

BARACK OBAMA

Dreams from My Father

A STORY OF RACE AND INHERITANCE

"Perceptive and wise, this book will tell you something about
yourself whether you are black or white."
—Marian Wright Edelman, author of *The Measure of Our Success*

The cover of Obama's autobiography, *Dreams from My Father: A Story of
Race and Inheritance* (Courtesy of AP Images/Seth Perlman)

poor neighborhoods, helping to give them a voice in elections. In the evenings, he also taught constitutional law classes at the University of Chicago's Law School. Teaching helped keep him sharp. As tough questions, such as abortion, gay rights, and affirmative action, landed in his lap, he became able to argue both sides. A popular teacher, Obama's students respected him for his intelligence and teaching ability.

Obama also finished writing his life story for the Crown Publishing Group, a division of Random House. The book, *Dreams from My Father: A Story of Race and Inheritance,* chronicled Obama's life from a young boy to the present. Published in 1995, the book told of Obama's struggles to discover his place in the world, his work as a community organizer, and his trip to Kenya.

Despite the success of having a book published, the year 1995 also was a sad one for Obama. His mother, Ann Dunham, died of ovarian cancer. He would miss her deeply. Her moral standards and activism had infused him. She also had exposed him to living abroad, giving him a more profound view of the world. Having family in underdeveloped countries, he couldn't ignore the sharp contrast between rich and poor people. His mother's beliefs had also helped him believe in himself. Pondering these values, and considering his legal work and political connections, Obama decided to step into the political world. He made no secret about wanting to run for political office, discussing it with his wife, his friends at Harvard, and at the law firm.

In 1996, when Obama was thirty-five years old, Illinois State senator Alice Palmer decided to run for a seat in the U.S. House of Representatives. This left a vacant seat and Obama decided not to run for her position as state senator.

Her district included both wealthy black and white families from the University of Chicago area, where Obama lived, and the poorer areas south of the city where he had worked as an organizer. As he fired up his campaign, Palmer changed her mind, having lost the primary election to represent her party. She wanted her job back, but Obama refused, saying she had promised not to run. Besides, his campaign was taking off. His workers challenged Palmer's petitions and won. She withdrew from the race, ending her career in politics.

Obama went to block club meetings, church socials, beauty and barber shops, and anywhere else he could find to share his views. He was often asked about his unusual name and why such a nice guy wanted to get into a nasty game like politics. He understood their skepticism; they both had seen politicians break their promises once they were elected. But he also saw another side to politics, stemming from the country's founding, and that side was his reason for running for office.

"We have a stake in one another, and that what binds us together is greater than that what drives us apart," he wrote. "And that if enough people believe in the truth of that proposition and act on it, then we might not solve every problem, but we can get something meaningful done."

Obama's youthful earnestness helped him to win a seat in the Illinois State Senate. His victory, however, left some hard feelings. Some politicians believed Obama should have stepped aside and let Palmer run for reelection. She was older and did not have as many chances to serve as he did.

Obama paid little attention to the criticism and set about fulfilling his duties as senator. He embraced the state of Illinois, seeing it as a microcosm of the country. It is "a rough

While serving as an Illinois state senator, Obama traveled the state, listening to people's concerns and opinions. *(Courtesy of AP Images/Seth Perlman)*

stew of North and South, East and West, urban and rural, black, white, and everything in between," he said. "Chicago may possess all the big-city sophistication of L.A. or New York, but geographically and culturally, the southern end of Illinois is closer to Little Rock or Louisville."

In 1997, during the summer after his first term as a state senator, Obama traveled around Illinois. He had no law school classes to teach and his wife was busy with her own work.

She had left Sidley & Austin to work in city government. Next, she led the Chicago arm of the national program Public Allies, a group encouraging young adults to pursue careers in public service. By 1996, she had become the associate dean of student services at the University of Chicago.

Obama took the road trip with his legislative aide, Dan Shomon. They traveled through cities and smaller towns, down Main Streets and past brick court houses. They passed shimmering blue lakes, golden corn fields, and roadside vendors selling warm, ripe peaches and fresh yellow corn. Each day they stopped to play golf. They dined at local restaurants and stopped at small coffee shops for some conversation and a slice of pie. Obama met both young and old people. It was a comfortable time, and he was sorry when it ended.

Obama enjoyed listening and was good at it. He had seen glimpses of people he remembered from his past: "In the faces of all the men and women I'd met I had recognized pieces of myself," he wrote. "In them I saw my grandfather's openness, my grandmother's matter-of-factness, my mother's kindness. The fried chicken, the potato salad, the grape halves in the Jell-O mold—all of it felt familiar."

For Obama, such trips kept him in touch with the people he represented in his state. With this knowledge in hand, he continued his work as a state senator. He also continued to teach law and was frequently invited to speak around town. He enjoyed these talks and the questions that arose from them. He heard questions about local, national, and international issues that kept him on his toes.

In 1999, Obama and his wife had their first child, a daughter they named Malia Ann. In the October following Malia's birth, Robinson took a part-time job working in the University of Chicago hospital system, and soon she became their vice president for community and external affairs.

A year after the birth of his daughter, Obama was faced with another political decision. He decided to run for U.S. Congress in the 2000 election cycle. He planned to unseat Bobby Rush, a four-term Democratic Congressman. Obama believed Rush wasn't doing enough for his district.

After he entered the race it seemed that everything that could go wrong did. Two weeks after Obama announced he was running, he had raised a few thousand dollars. In a poll, Rush's name recognition was 90 percent, while Obama's was 11 percent. Rush's approval rating was 70 percent, while Obama's was 8 percent.

In October, Rush's adult son was shot by drug dealers outside of his house. Obama respectfully suspended his campaign for a month. At Christmas, he traveled to Hawaii with his wife and daughter, planning to spend the holiday with Toot. During their visit, the Illinois state legislature called for a special vote on a gun control law. Malia was sick and unable to fly. Obama missed the vote, and the bill failed. The *Chicago Tribune* ran a front page story about the bill's failure and Obama's failure to get back for the important vote.

Obama had no choice but to grimly follow through with the campaign, although he knew he had no chance of winning. Rush beat him by a two-to-one margin in the primary. Critics called it disastrous. Obama retreated to his civil rights firm, which he'd neglected during his campaign. His political career had left him with little money.

Friends decided he needed some political therapy and convinced Obama to attend the Democratic Convention in 2000. They hoped it would help him get over his loss. Obama

After losing his bid for a U.S. congressional seat in 2000, a humiliated and dejected Obama was forced to watch Al Gore's Democratic National Convention speech on television. *(Courtesy of AP Images/Ron Edmonds)*

arrived at the airport only to have his American Express card rejected at the Hertz rental counter. After a half and hour on the phone, a kindly supervisor authorized his car rental. But Obama had no credentials as a delegate and there were no floor passes available for the convention. Instead, he watched the Democratic Party nominate Al Gore on television. He left with a bitter memory of the experience.

Later Obama wrote that his defeat in 2000 was, "the

sort of drubbing that awakens you to the fact that life is not obliged to work out as you'd planned."

Obama had described political candidates as being locked in a grip of fear that refused to release them until after Election Day. He now knew this was because a candidate's loss often left one burning with humiliation. But Obama learned from his experience. Despite his competitive and impatient spirit, he decided to take things more slowly. He was driven, yet he needed to compromise and learn to wait.

six

A Rising Star

*D*espite his painful loss to Bobby Rush, Obama threw himself back into his work. The years were happy, if busy, ones. In 2001, Obama and his wife had a second daughter. They named her Natasha, calling her Sasha for short.

Over his next years in the Illinois state senate Obama helped to pass several laws. He introduced more than 780 bills, about 280 of which became laws. He had a hand in reforming the death penalty system. A number of death row inmates had been found innocent. Obama pushed legislation that required confessions and interrogations be videotaped, protecting both law enforcement and the accused. He also advocated the expansion of early childhood education. Through his work with the state's health care program, 20,000 additional children and 65,000 more families were insured. Another one of his bills further protected women from abuse. Families across Illinois benefited too from the

Earned Income Tax Credit that in three years returned 100 million dollars in tax cuts to those who needed it most. Obama learned how to work with both Democrats and Republicans, and to weigh both points of view.

Then in April of 2003, Obama saw another chance to advance his political career. Illinois's U.S. senator, Peter Fitzgerald decided not to run for a second term. Fitzgerald had spent 19 million dollars of his own personal fortune to unseat the previous senator, Carol Moseley Braun. But he was not widely popular and didn't seem to enjoy politics.

Despite his previous loss, the forty-two-year-old Obama was ready to try again, with the somewhat reluctant support of his wife. They already had busy lives, with two young children and full-time jobs. Obama's wife balanced most of the work, coordinating her own job with raising their two daughters. Even so, she suggested her husband give it a shot, although she jokingly warned that he "shouldn't necessarily count on her vote."

Obama faced six other Democratic opponents in the primary. He announced his candidacy in January of 2003. At first it was hard to get attention. Often no reporters came when Obama's four young staffers and ten volunteers called press conferences. When they signed up to be in Chicago's St. Patrick's Day Parade, they got the last slot in the parade. "[M]y ten volunteers and I found ourselves marching just a few paces ahead of the city's sanitation trucks, waving to the few stragglers who remained on the route while workers swept up garbage and peeled green shamrock stickers off the lampposts," Obama wrote.

Running for statewide office required a lot of money. While it couldn't guarantee a victory or buy passion or charisma, not having enough money guaranteed failure. Money bought more media coverage; one week of television advertising in Chicago cost half a million dollars. Four weeks of television coverage, plus money to pay staffers and cover expenses, would cost up to 5 million dollars for the primary alone. They would need to raise at least 10 million dollars. Obama sat down and wrote a list of everyone he thought might contribute. He would have to find wealthy donors. He was campaigning against Blair Hull, a shy campaigner, but a man with endless money. Hull had sold his financial trading business for 53 million dollars.

David Axelrod, Obama's media consultant, spelled out their strategy. They would need to count on grassroots campaigning techniques and "earned media," meaning the ability to make their own news.

Obama drove from county to county, from town to town, crossing train tracks and passing miles of corn and bean fields. He relied on friends, religious groups, and acquaintances who set up visits to groups, churches, and clubs. After long hours of driving, he sometimes found two or three people gathered around a kitchen table to meet him. No matter how many people attended, Obama listened.

"I tried my best to keep my mouth shut and hear what they had to say," Obama said. "I listened to people talk about their jobs, their businesses, the local school; their anger at Bush and their anger at Democrats; their dogs, their back pain, their war service, and the things they remembered from their childhood."

The simplicity of people's hopes struck Obama. They believed if people were willing to work, they should be paid a living wage. They also believed that every child should have a good education, and that college tuition should be affordable, along with health care. They wanted to be safe—from not only terrorists and criminals, but also from pollution. Regardless of race, age, or religion, most people held these values. Obama agreed with them, which prompted him to work harder than he ever had.

Although, it was a cash strapped, grassroots campaign, Obama quickly shot ahead of the other Democrats. In March of 2004, he won the primary by 53 percent of the vote. Obama had connected with people and had already proven during his two terms as state senator that he could get things done.

As he entered the general election it first looked like Obama had an almost insurmountable challenge before him. The Republican nominee, Jack Ryan, was wealthy and well-funded. But soon after the primary he self-destructed because of a family scandal. The Republicans had difficulty

Obama debates with his Republican opponent Alan Keyes during the 2004 U.S. Senate race. *(Courtesy of AP Images/Jeff Roberson)*

finding a new candidate and finally brought in Alan Keyes from Maryland. Keyes was an arch conservative with a Ph.D from Harvard. He was also African American, which is one of the reasons the Illinois Republicans thought he would be a formidable candidate against Obama. Keyes had run for president in 2000, and this was his second run for a seat in the U.S. Senate. He had never won an election, and never lived in Illinois.

As soon as he entered the race Keyes began to attack Obama on his character, his ideas, and his religion. He seemed to say whatever popped into his mind. Before long he had insulted nearly everyone, even many who agreed with his religious and political positions. Illinois Republicans soon realized they had blundered by importing Keyes from Maryland.

The Republican Party also assigned a young man to track Obama's public appearances, a fairly common tactic. But the young man was a bit too zealous, tailing Obama from the morning to night. He remained about five to ten feet away with his video camera, following Obama to the bathroom, in elevators, and even when he was on his cell phone with his wife and children.

First, Obama tried reasoning with his tail. When that failed, he went to the media and introduced the man to them. This let the public know he was being stalked and this invasion of his privacy became a campaign issue. The Republican Party apologized, but the damage had been done.

Obama realized that Keyes was truly the ideal candidate. Given time, Keyes would defeat himself by generating his own negative press. Obama's integrity and his positive campaign slogan "Yes, we can," clashed with Keyes's mudslinging tactics. "All I had to do was keep my mouth shut and start planning my swearing-in ceremony," Obama later joked.

Obama's campaign eventually raised 14 million dollars—impressive for a virtually unknown candidate who faced a weak challenger. One of his personal heroes, Michael Jordan, contributed $10,000. Obama became increasingly popular and began to speak in different states on behalf of other candidates.

He still got questions about his name. After the terrorist attacks of September 11, 2001, being named Obama seemed like a political liability. His name was just one letter different from that of terrorist leader Osama Bin Laden. His middle name, Hussein, like the former Iraqi dictator, Saddam Hussein, didn't score any points either.

"People call me 'Alabama.' They call me 'Your Mama,'" Obama joked. But others didn't see it as a joking matter. One Web site featured a picture of Osama Bin Laden with Obama's face superimposed on top. The picture was taken down, and an apology issued. But his name caught people's attention at other times too.

Jan Schakowsky, a member of the Illinois congressional delegation, recalled wearing an Obama button on a visit to the White House. When President George Bush glimpsed the button "he jumped back, almost literally," Schakowsky said. She knew what he was thinking and explained that this was a button for Obama with a "B," and that he was running for the U.S. Senate.

"Well, I don't know him," Bush said.

"But you will, Mr. President," she replied.

The scene that first brought Obama to the attention of Americans outside of Illinois occurred during the 2004 Democratic National Convention in July. He was asked to

Obama delivers a stirring speech to a crowd of supporters during the 2004 Democratic National Convention. *(Courtesy of AP Images/Charlie Neibergall)*

give the keynote address. There would be 35,000 people in the audience, and millions more watching on television and on the internet. This was a huge honor—and opportunity—for a relative newcomer. Standing in the wings before the speech, Robinson calmed her jittery husband, breaking the tension with laughter when she looked into Obama's eyes and said, "Just don't screw it up buddy."

In a stirring speech, Obama spoke of the country's problems, and the divisions that smothered dreams for families and children. He tugged at emotions when he talked about the war in Iraq. He spoke of his own parents and their different cultures, but how this great country could also be unified.

"I say tonight . . . there's not a black America and white America and Latino America and Asian America. There's a United States of America," he told the audience. "In the end, that is (the) greatest gift to us . . . the bedrock of this nation; the belief in things not seen; the belief that there are better days ahead."

His words of hope stirred the crowd. They roared with approval at his final words.

The speech rocketed him into national political fame. It impressed both Democrats and Republicans. Some called it one of the greatest political convention keynote addresses in memory. "He is without a doubt the most dynamic speaker up there," another candidate's aide ruefully commented. "I wish my candidate had half that."

Obama's popularity soared. He was elected to the U.S. Senate, winning more than 70 percent of the vote. Barack Obama became the third black senator in history.

Obama's book *Dreams from My Father,* which had previously attracted little attention, was reprinted and jumped to the top of the *New York Times* bestseller list, where it remained for forty weeks, spending four consecutive weeks as number one. Thousands of tickets were sold for book signings, breaking records set earlier by former U.S. President Bill Clinton. Crown Publishing Group offered Obama a deal to write three more books. His advances totaled 1.9 million dollars. He would write two books for adults and one for children. He planned to work on the children's book with his wife and daughters, donating the proceeds to charity. The book would share his experiences as a skinny kid, with big ears, and a funny name who grew up to be a U.S. senator.

Along with the book signings, invitations poured in for Obama to speak. The NAACP awarded him the Fight for Freedom Award and the Chairman's Award, recognizing his special achievements and distinguished service.

Yet for all of the awards and recognition, Obama still had a job to do. In January of 2004, when he arrived in Washington D.C. for his swearing-in ceremony as a U.S. senator, he soon realized how inexperienced he was. He was lucky that Keyes had launched a dirty campaign that people

Obama celebrates after being elected as a U.S. senator. *(Courtesy of AP Images/M. Spencer Green)*

reacted strongly against. In other places across the country, most Democrats weren't so lucky. They had lost the presidency, seats in the House, and seats in the Senate. "I felt like the rookie who shows up after the game, his uniform spotless, eager to play, even as his mud-splattered teammates tend to their wounds."

During his campaign, Obama had made good use of the internet, increasing his status with younger voters. Some Web sites called him the "Great Black Hope," while others sold "Obama for President" and "Obama in 2012" posters and bumper stickers.

In Kenya, the response was echoed. Many people there had similar hopes for Obama. African parents named their

A Kenyan man holds a painting of Obama inscribed with the words, "Welcome home" during Obama's 2006 return visit to Kenya. *(Courtesy of AP Images/Sayyid Azim)*

Obama poses with his wife and daughters, Malia (left) and Sasha, after taking the Senate oath from Vice President Dick Cheney. *(Courtesy of AP Images/Lawrence Jackson)*

babies Barack. They held Obama up as a role model for their children and even named an elementary school after him.

Obama had seen the White House in 1984 when Ronald Reagan was president. He had just graduated from college, and President Reagan was proposing a cut in student aid. Obama worked with student leaders, many of them black, Puerto Rican, and Eastern European who were the first in their families to attend college, rounding up petitions against the cuts. Obama delivered the petitions to the New York congressional delegation. During that visit, he walked the mall, stared up at the towering white column of the Washington Monument, and gazed at the White House. He never realized that one day he would see the inside of the White House, with its walls steeped in history. Months after his election he saw the Lincoln bedroom, complete with antique furniture, an original copy of the Gettysburg Address, and a big flat-screen TV on a desk.

"Who, I wondered, flipped on *Sports Center* while spending the night in the Lincoln Bedroom?" he wrote.

On January 4, 2005, Obama was sworn in to the 109th Congress. His friends and relatives from Illinois, Hawaii, London, and Kenya crowded the Senate gallery. His daughters, in their pink and flowered dresses, did their part too. Six-year-old Malia shook hands with Vice President Dick Cheney, while three-year-old Sasha slapped his palm, before twirling around to face the cameras. Outside in the bright winter sunshine, a few hundred well-wishers stood by for hugs, handshakes, and autographs.

Inside the Senate Chamber there are columns of marble and its creamy white oval ceiling emblazoned with a Bald Eagle. One hundred mahogany desks, arranged in a horseshoe shape sat ready. Some of the desks dated back to 1819, atop each a receptacle for inkwells and quills. Written inside each desk's drawer were the names of the previous senators who sat at that desk. Obama would sit at Robert F. Kennedy's desk.

In Obama's first month he was busy hiring new staffers, setting up offices in Washington, D.C., and Illinois, answering 10,000 letters from constituents, and responding to three hundred speaking invitations each week. In addition, he needed to keep up with his schedule. There's a saying senators use when asked to describe their first year on Capitol Hill: "It's like drinking from a fire hose."

Many people feared that the fame and hype Obama was received would sour other senators toward their new colleague.

In January of 2005, *Newsweek* magazine featured him on the cover as a Democrat to watch. Obama humbly reminded everyone that he was number ninety-nine out of one hundred senators. He quipped that his new status would require him to sharpen pencils and clean the Capitol building's latrines. But his modesty only increased the demand for him to speak at Democratic Party fundraisers.

Obama traveled around the country, quickly raising $1.8 million. He also formed the Hopefund, a political committee to help elect Democratic leaders. The committee's goal was to elect people who believed that government must invest in the community, provide tax breaks to reward the creation of jobs, curb the abuses of health care, and defend human liberties at home and abroad.

As a part of the Hopefund, Obama also organized Yes We Can, a job training and placement program, inspired by his days as a community organizer. The program was designed to recruit and train young people of color to work on political campaigns. This would create talented campaign staffers experienced in many areas of political campaigning who would continue working in politics for a long time.

Despite his work, Obama was also adjusting to living alone. He and his wife had decided that she and their daughters would remain in Chicago. They had a support system there and didn't want to uproot the girls. Obama would fly home to Chicago on the weekends, treading a delicate balance between his work and his family, while also dealing with his newfound celebrity status. This was not always easy.

One such time when Obama had to juggle two important events was during his first year as a senator. The Florida

Democratic Party invited him to speak at a dinner. Waiters poured wine and served the salad. Obama was on a jet from Midway Airport in Chicago after watching his daughters' holiday ballet recital. He made it to the dinner and spoke, being able to attend both events, with a little creative scheduling.

Obama and his wife tried to keep Sundays as a private family time. It was a day for hearing about school activities, reading, going to the movies, taking walks, spending time with their daughters, and catching up in their family journal. Sometimes at night, Obama read *Harry Potter* books to his daughters. At home, Obama helped with grocery shopping, made beds, and took out the trash.

Despite his hectic, dizzying, and sometimes frustrating schedule, Obama was fascinated with his new job. He soon established a rhythm of life, leaving Chicago on Monday night or Tuesday morning, depending on the Senate's voting schedule. He made a daily trip to the Senate gym, and occasionally met a friend for lunch or dinner. He spent the rest of his week giving speeches, attending committee meetings and fundraisers, and making phone calls. He wrote letters, reviewed legislation, and drafted op-eds. He attended policy briefings, an endless series of meetings, and hosted constituent coffees. On Thursday evenings, after he got word of when the last vote of the week would be, he cast his vote, headed down the Capitol steps, and hoped to catch the next flight to Chicago, making it home before his two daughters fell asleep.

Focusing on his constituents, he pressed for additional payments for Illinois veterans. He also pushed for $2.5 billion for locks and dams projects on Illinois rivers. He threatened to block nominees to the Environmental Protection Agency until they passed new regulations for lead paint, a particular worry in Chicago homes.

Obama formed partnerships both internationally and with members of both the Democratic and Republican Parties. As a senator, he was the first to speak out on the threat of avian flu, helping pass an amendment to aid the World Health Organization response to a potential flu pandemic. He also advanced a measure to increase ethanol production, giving tax credits to gas stations that installed ethanol fuel pumps. He focused on immigration reform, and scrutinized government contracts with companies to help victims of Hurricane Katrina. Obama also visited Russia with Senator Richard Lugar from Indiana. The two of them inspected stockpiles of nuclear weapons.

Obama also became a critic of the U.S. President George W. Bush and his administration. While he disagreed with many of the president's decisions, he didn't see Bush as a bad man. The president was only doing what he thought was best. However, Obama saw some of the consequences of the administration's actions that he disliked.

"Whenever I write a letter to a family who has lost a loved one in Iraq, or read an email from a constituent who has dropped out of college because her student aid has been cut, I'm reminded that the actions of those in power have enormous consequences—a price that they themselves almost never have to pay," Obama wrote.

For these reasons, similar to those of his community organizer days, Obama opposed the president's tax cuts, saying that they were financially and morally troubling because the wealthiest got the biggest cut. He also highlighted the lack of a meaningful health care policy and no serious energy

Obama and George W. Bush greet each other. *(Courtesy of AP Images/Pablo Martinez Monsivais)*

policy. Overall, he questioned the administration's faulty evidence of weapons of mass destruction in Iraq, and the ultimate U.S. invasion.

Obama had approved it when, within a week after the terrorist attacks of September 11, 2001, the Senate voted 98-0 to give the president the power to use appropriate force against the nations behind the attacks. The Bush administration drove the Taliban government out of Kabul, Afghanistan, wreaking havoc on Al Qaeda terrorists who had planned the terrorist attacks on September 11. But Obama was disappointed in the administration's lack of coordinated planning. To him, the policies were cobbled together and outdated.

When President Bush led the United States to war against Iraq, as the next front in the war on terror, Obama did not think it was the right course of action. The United States had little international support for the invasion and he believed the reasoning behind the war was unconvincing. In October of 2002, he had spoken to a crowd of 2,000 people gathered in front of Chicago's Federal Plaza. He didn't support "a dumb war, a rash war, a war based not on reason but on passion, not on principle but on politics," Obama had said. "I know that even a successful war against Iraq will require a U.S. occupation of undetermined length, at undetermined cost, with undetermined consequences." He worried that such a war without international support would only worsen problems in the Middle East.

Obama's speech was well received. It gave him a reputation of not being afraid to speak out on tough issues. At that time Obama didn't know if he was correct. He suspected he might be wrong when U.S. forces marched through Baghdad, toppling a statue of dictator Saddam Hussein, and suffering few casualties. However, three years later, American deaths had risen to more than 3,000, with at least 16,000 soldiers wounded, and tens of thousands of Iraqi deaths. The war had cost $250 billion, with billions more expected, and there was no end in sight. The cost had created years of debt to pay off, along with the costs of providing care for injured veterans. It had also increased international anti-American sentiment and allowed Afghanistan to slip in chaos.

In 2006, Obama visited Iraq in a military cargo plane. Fitted in a Kevlar vest and helmet, his blood type recorded in case of an accident, he viewed worn and battered Baghdad from a U.S. Blackhawk helicopter. What he saw led him to support a withdrawal of U.S. troops by the end of 2008, believing the situation to have disintegrated into a low grade civil war between different factions. His approach differed from that of the president, who had suggested sending more troops in an attempt to finish the war decisively. Questions still abounded about the future of U.S. involvement in Iraq.

When Senator Obama was not traveling internationally, he enjoyed hosting town hall meetings across Illinois, from the state's prosperous suburbs to its smaller towns. He traveled to both rural and urban areas, meeting with anywhere from fifty to 2,000 people. Sometimes they discussed local issues, at other times he fielded questions about prescription drug programs, avian flu, and the country's space program. People slipped him notes, business cards, and even pressed good luck charms into his hand. The message he saw in people's faces is *Don't disappoint us.*

This message was reflected overseas too, in Kenya. In 2006, nineteen years after his last visit to his father's country, he traveled there again, this time with his wife and daughters. Thousands of people gathered to see him and his family. In Nairobi, people stood on rooftops, peered from windows, and lined the streets to greet him.

"He's a hero, and people are really expecting much from him," said Benjamin Okola, a member of the Luo tribe and taxi driver in Nairobi.

During Obama's fifteen day tour, he visited with relatives. He also spent time learning more about the spread of AIDS, avian flu, and other diseases that plagued Africa. Obama heard about the impact of climate change on the continent, and traveled to different parts of Africa. Everywhere he was met with the same high expectations. Dr. Obama's son had returned in a blaze of glory. Everyone wondered what he would accomplish next.

seven

Together We Can

Before the midterm elections in November of 2006, Obama finished his second book, *The Audacity of Hope: Thoughts on Reclaiming the American Dream.* He had won a Grammy Award for the recording of his other book, *Dreams of My Father: A Story of Race and Inheritance.* His reading of the book had won the Best Spoken Word Album category as an audio book, beating out fellow nominee Bob Dylan.

Obama's second book was released on October 16, 2006. Within one month it sold 750,000 copies and was chosen as one of the top books of 2006. By the end of February 2007, the book had spent seventeen weeks on the *New York Times* bestseller list.

When Obama went on a book tour fans lined up in front of bookstores. They flocked to hear the senator speak. Customers lined up to buy "Obama for President" buttons and "He's ready. Why wait. Obama '08" bumper stickers from enterprising vendors. Obama had achieved rock star

Obama signs a book during his tour for *The Audacity of Hope*. *(Courtesy of AP Images/Charles Rex Arbogast)*

status. After the election, a big success for the Democratic Party, many of his supporters quipped that Obama's adoring fans were Barack-and-rollers.

"We originally scheduled the Rolling Stones for this party," said New Hampshire governor John Lynch when introducing Obama in Manchester, New Hampshire. "But we cancelled them when we realized that Senator Obama would sell more tickets."

Amidst his soaring popularity, Obama continued to meet with his senior staff and informal advisors. They assembled periodically, holding evening sessions, setting strategies, and appraising Obama's performance. In November of 2006, they held a four-hour session, with stacks of take-out pizza. They gathered in a conference room to talk about the senator's future.

Many people wondered if Barack Obama was thinking about running for president of the United States.

"Sometimes a book tour is more than just a book tour," said a former aide of Vice President Al Gore. "Senator Obama appears to be using the book to really test presidential winds."

Others across the country encouraged Obama to run for president.

"Run, Barack, Run," wrote David Brooks of the *New York Times.* "Barack Obama should run for president. He should run first for the good of his party. It would demoralize the Democrats to go through a long primary season with the most exciting figure in the party looming off in the distance like some unapproachable dream."

Three months later, many people's wishes seemed to come true. On the anniversary of what would have been Martin Luther King Jr.'s seventy-eighth birthday, Barack Obama filed papers with the Federal Election Commission and set up an exploratory committee to consider a run for the presidency. On his Web site, he released a videotaped message to his supporters, explaining his decision. He had heard over and over the premise that the nation was hungry for new and fresh leadership. He wanted to know if they thought he was the man who could deliver that leadership.

After the announcement, in the early hours of that January morning, hundreds of people called Obama's preliminary campaign operation. They offered their services and gave a flood of responses. Their enthusiasm swamped the campaign.

Obama's start sparked a flurry of media attention as well. He knew about the difficulty of running a campaign for president. Besides the incredible stress, all aspects of his life would become cause for public attention and comment. People questioned his race, his religion, his experience, and his age.

As for religion, Obama said he found great comfort in his own religion and deep faith. For years, he and his family had attended Chicago's Trinity United Church of Christ, where he and his wife were married. Obama was raised with exposure to many different religions, and he focused on respecting all faiths in the nation. "Whatever we once were, we are no longer just a Christian nation," he wrote. "We are also a Jewish nation, a Muslim nation, a Buddhist nation, a Hindu nation, and a nation of nonbelievers."

Obama also understood the skepticism about his experience and people's comments that he had not been in Washington, D.C., long enough to know the ropes of government. He had only been serving in the U.S. Senate since his election in November of 2004. He faced other senators with more experiences. Hillary Clinton had served for two terms as a senator from New York, and also as first lady for eight years, when her husband was president. Senator John McCain also had more senatorial experience and had served admirably during the Vietnam War.

"War hero against snot-nosed rookie," was how Obama jokingly suggested a campaign might be run against him by McCain.

Doubts were expressed over Obama's political inexperience in comparison to other presidential candidates such as Senator Hillary Clinton (left). *(Courtesy of AP Images/Evan Vucci)*

In earnest response to the questions of his experience, Obama responded simply that he had been in government long enough to know that the ways of Washington, D.C., must change.

Some agreed that Obama's age was in his favor, as he would be forty-seven by the time he was elected president. He would be thirteen years younger than fellow Democratic candidate Hillary Clinton and twenty-five years younger than Republican candidate John McCain.

"There's something to be said for a politician who didn't come of age wearing sideburns and listening to Simon and Garfunkel," commented Jennifer Senior, in an article in the *New Yorker*.

Funding for a presidential run was a huge challenge. The cost of contending in a presidential election increased from year to year. In 2004, George W. Bush had spent more than $367 million to win. People estimated that to at least win the Democratic Party nomination in 2008, Obama would need at least $50 million. Some of his opponents would probably raise $100 million or more.

Raising such funds would certainly be a challenge. But Obama had a habit of rooting for the underdog—from his community organizer days to his fondness for the Chicago White Sox. In 2005, the team, perennial losers, finally captured their first World Series title since 1917. Obama, a southpaw, threw out the first pitch in one of their playoff games.

Obama carefully weighed all of these factors when considering his decision whether to run for president. He planned to make his final decision surrounded by friends and family. He and his wife and daughters took a trip to Hawaii for a week and a half. They would return to Washington, D.C., the first week of January. He planned no public events or interviews—only enjoyed the ocean, played golf and basketball with his buddies, and pondered one of the biggest questions he would ever face, discussing the pros and cons with the most important people in his life.

"It's a much needed time for reflection," said his sister Maya, now Maya Soetoro-Ng. "He's got to figure out what he's going to do."

Obama throws the ceremonial first pitch during a playoff game between the Chicago White Sox and the Los Angeles Angels. *(Courtesy of AP Images/ Ann Heisenfelt)*

Obama announces his bid for presidency of the United States in front of the Old State Capitol building in Springfield, Illinois. *(Courtesy of AP Photo/Charles Rex Arbogast)*

On February 10, 2007, Barack Obama made the announcement that people across the nation and overseas had been waiting to hear. In the shadow of the domed, white-columned Old State Capitol building in Springfield, Illinois, he announced his bid for the presidency of the United States. A crowd of 15,000 people gathered in the frigid ten degrees Fahrenheit weather to hear his momentous speech. The speech opened to the strains of a U2 song, "City of Blinding Lights," as Obama humbly welcomed cheering fans to the long and uncertain road on which he was about to embark. He called on this campaign not to only be about him, but about people striving to improve their country.

"Few obstacles can withstand the power of millions of voices calling for change," Obama said. "By ourselves, this change will not happen. Divided, we are bound to fail. But the life of a tall, gangly, self-made Springfield lawyer tells us that a different future is possible. He tells us that there is power in words. He tells us that there is power in conviction," Obama continued, drawing on the memory of Abraham Lincoln.

In his speech, Obama reminded the audience of the current challenges that faced the United States: the war in Iraq had no end in sight, schools had too many children not learning, families struggled paycheck to paycheck, climate change threatened the future, along with a dependence on foreign oil, and health care costs strained incomes. The problems continued, he said, because of the pettiness of politicians and a failure of leadership.

Revealing his platform to the crowd, he called for an end to the war in Iraq, while still fighting terrorism by destroying the world's deadliest weapons, improving army intelligence, and rebuilding world alliances. Obama also pledged to tackle the health care crisis and invest in scientific research. He called for increased standards in schools, providing more resources to schools, and making college tuition affordable. Furthermore, he advocated for an end to poverty by strengthening job training and through offering affordable child care. He suggested addressing global warming by studying alternative fuels and fuel efficient cars.

The response to his message was phenomenal. In the two weeks after the campaign kicked off, 3,306 grassroots volunteer groups formed, attracting tens of thousands of members who organized both on- and off-line. By the end of the first quarter of 2007, he had raised $25.8 million, and on his campaign Web site, 38,799 people networked with others in communities across the country, planning events and sharing why they supported Obama.

Obama reminded everyone that change, while necessary, isn't easy. Many people chose to focus on the divisions in society, while he choses to believe that "beneath all the differences of race and region, faith and station, we are one people. . . . there is power in hope."

eight
From Dream to Reality

As the 2008 election year drew near, it became clear that the two front-runners to secure the Democratic Party's nomination were Barack Obama and Hillary Clinton. Clinton had raised the most money and received the most endorsements from powerful Democratic politicians. Many pundits saw her as the candidate to beat.

Soon, though, Obama proved that he could also raise money and draw huge crowds to his political rallies. But the expectation that Clinton would be the Democratic nominee for president remained a huge obstacle. At one point he was almost thirty points behind in the polls.

However, his aides in the campaign noticed that Obama didn't seem worried. His composure gave them confidence. By the end of the year it appeared his confidence was beginning to pay-off. Reporters who followed the campaign began to notice that Obama was drawing larger crowds than Clinton and the contributions to his campaign, many received through his Web site and outreach program, began to pour in at a faster rate.

Primaries and caucuses—where party voters elect which delegates will be sent to party's national convention—began early in 2008. Ideally, whichever candidate is able to send more delegates to the convention will get the nomination— but in 2008, the battle for delegates turned into a long and drawn-out process.

The first challenge was the Iowa caucuses, held on January 3, 2008. With her large campaign and ample support, Clinton seemed poised to sweep the Iowa caucuses. A decisive victory in Iowa would have won Clinton a great deal of momentum and made it difficult for any of the other candidates to over- take her.

Obama surprised everyone, though, including the Clinton campaign, when he won in Iowa. Clinton's campaign managers had underestimated how many new people would participate in the caucuses over 2004, new voters who overwhelmingly supported Obama.

A week later, at the New Hampshire primary, Clinton proved she was resilient and won a decisive victory. It was becoming clear that the battle for the Democratic presiden- tial nomination was going to be hard fought.

Obama won the next primary, in South Carolina. The pattern of Obama and Clinton switching off victories con- tinued until February 16. There were so many primaries and caucuses that day the press dubbed it Super Tuesday. Clinton hoped to sweep the Super Tuesday elections, and wrap up the nomination. Instead, Obama split the day with her, winning nearly as many of the individual state elections and delegates.

After Super Tuesday, Obama won eleven consecutive primaries and caucuses. At the end of his string of victories he had accumulated so many more delegates than Clinton that his lead appeared insurmountable. Regardless, the campaign continued. There was a great deal of speculation among the press and other politicians that the contest between Clinton and Obama would become so negative that the bad feelings would destroy either candidates' chance of defeating Arizona senator John McCain, the Republican presidential nominee, in November.

Ultimately, though, Clinton conceded defeat on June 3, 2008, the last day of the primary season. On that day, Obama secured enough delegates to be selected at the National

Obama engaged in debate with Senator Hillary Rodham Clinton during the February 21, 2008, Democratic presidential debate in Austin, Texas. (*Courtesy of AP Images*)

Democratic Convention, to be held in less than two months in Denver, Colorado.

After the drawn-out and often bitter contest of the primaries, Obama worked to secure the support of Clinton and her supporters. Many of her supporters were disappointed that their long-held dream of a woman president had been delayed yet again. Obama's mission, which continued until November, was to convince her supporters he would do his best to represent all people, regardless of race and gender. Many were eventually convinced, especially after Clinton endorsed and began campaigning for Obama.

Soon after securing the nomination, Obama took an overseas trip to visit the American troops stationed in Europe and those fighting in the Iraq War. On the way back to the United States he stopped in Berlin, Germany, and gave a

Obama taking an aerial tour of Baghdad, Iraq, with U.S. Army General David Petraeus (right) on July 21, 2008. *(Courtesy of U.S. Dept. of Defense/Staff Sgt. Lorie Jewell)*

speech to more than 100,000 people. Clearly, the prospect of America electing Obama to the presidency had excited people all over the world.

Obama's next big decision was to select a vice-presidential candidate to run with him in the fall. After interviewing several people, including governors and senators, he chose Senator Joe Biden from Delaware. Biden had been a candidate for the nomination but had dropped out early. A senator since 1973, Biden was considered an authority on foreign policy. By choosing him, Obama hoped to convince voters that although he wasn't as experienced in foreign policy as Senator McCain, he had selected a knowledgeable man to be at his side.

The Obama campaign worked extra hard to make the Democratic Convention, held in late July, a resounding success. It planned something different from previous conventions on the final night. Before, the presidential nominee had given his acceptance speech inside the hall where the convention was being held. Instead, Obama's team decided to hold the final night, when Obama's speech was to be

Joe Biden *(Courtesy of United States Senate)*

delivered, at Denver's Invesco Field. A crowd of more than 70,000 people gathered to hear him lay out his plans for the future and to challenge McCain to run a campaign centered on the issues.

Obama gives his acceptance speech at Invesco Field in Denver, Colorado, after securing the Democratic nomination for president. *(Courtesy of AP Images)*

The day after Obama's acceptance speech, John McCain excited the nation by selecting Governor Sarah Palin of Alaska as his running mate. She was a forceful advocate of Republican principles. In addition, her image as a moose hunting advocate of rugged individualism appealed to many voters. Her selection gave McCain a boost in the polls.

The campaigns began meeting to arrange for the three presidential debates and one vice-presidential debate. But a few days before the first debate took place outside events changed the political atmosphere and what was at stake in the election.

The leaders of American banks, as well as the chairman of the Federal Reserve System, which has the task of controlling how much money is circulating in the economy and of helping to keep banks solvent, announced that the entire financial system of the United States was about to collapse. One after another, the largest financial companies in the country announced that they were on the brink of bankruptcy.

When the news broke, Senator McCain first told reporters that he was certain the fundamentals of our economy were strong. Then he announced that he would not participate in the first presidential debate. Instead, he was going to Washington, D.C., to help bring the crisis to an end. He challenged Obama to do the same.

Obama refused to go along with canceling the debate. He said that a president had to be able to handle more than one crisis at a time and that he would be at the debate, to be held in Florida, and hoped McCain would join him.

McCain's reaction to the crisis ended up hurting him in the polls. While Obama looked cool under the pressure, McCain came across to some as agitated. There was also the suspicion that he was trying to use the problem to his political advantage. He was further hurt when his efforts to arrive at a quick solution failed. In the end, he was on the stage with Obama for the debate.

Obama prepared intensely before the first debate. McCain had been in national politics for decades, and was a formidable and respected opponent. He knew it was important for him to be prepared, to convince Americans he had the steadiness and knowledge to be a successful president.

The first debate was about foreign policy, considered to be McCain's strongest area. He had served in Congress since 1982 and had spent more than five years in a prisoner of war camp during the Vietnam War. However, because of the recent financial crisis, the debate's focus largely shifted to economic questions instead of those about foreign policy.

After the debate, public opinion polls indicated that many felt Obama had come out on top. This same pattern held for the other two debates. Obama showed voters he was ready to be president. He knew citizens wanted a change in how their government was run and Obama was convincing them he was the man for the job.

The one big question looming over the campaign was race. So far it had not seemed to be decisive, except for

In this October 7, 2008, photo, Obama answers a question as John McCain listens during a town hall-style presidential debate at Belmont University. After the debate, polls indicated that Obama had come out on top. (*Courtesy of AP Images*)

one incident. During the primary campaign against Hillary Clinton a tape had been released of Obama's minister, Reverend Jeremiah Wright, castigating the United States for a history of slavery and racism from his church's pulpit. Obama had weathered that storm by delivering a thoughtful and moving speech about race. Now there was fear the tape would again be used to frighten voters. There was also a more general fear that at the last moment a majority of Americans would decide not to vote for an African American. By mid-October it seemed fairly certain that if this did not happen, Obama would be elected the forty-fourth president of the United States.

Obama's campaign worked to counter this possibility, and any other scenario that would hurt Obama, by developing the most sophisticated "get out the vote" campaign ever seen in American politics. Thousands of people volunteered to knock on doors, make telephone calls, and contribute money.

By election day, no polls indicated that Obama's race would keep him out of the White House. The polls were right. On election day, November 4, 2008, Barack Obama was elected president. The United States had entered a new era. Many Americans, especially ones old enough to remember the racial strife of the 1960s and 1970s, were surprised that the majority of voting Americans were ready to put some of that ugly past behind them.

After voting in his hometown of Chicago, Obama spent the day with his family. That night, after the networks called Obama as the victor, Senator McCain made a gracious concession speech. Then, Obama, Michelle, and their daughters appeared on a stage set up in Chicago's Grant Park. He told the crowd, "it has been a long time coming, but tonight,

Obama, his wife Michelle, and their two daughters wave to a crowd of supporters in Chicago, Illinois, after Obama's victory in the presidential election. *(Courtesy of AP Images)*

because of what we did on this day, in this election, at this defining moment, change has come to America."

Unfortunately, one of Obama's biggest supporters never got to see that historic moment. Just two days before the election, on November 2, Obama's grandmother, Madelyn Dunham, died of cancer at the age of eighty-six. Obama had known she was ill—two weeks earlier he'd suspended his campaign for two days to spend time with her—but her passing added a bittersweet note to the end of the campaign. Speaking about "Toot," as he called her, after her death, the usually reserved Obama dabbed at tears in his eyes, and praised his grandmother as an example of strength and stability in his life.

In his inaugural address on January 20, 2009, President Obama faced a crowd estimated to be around 2 million people. They had come from all over the U.S. and beyond, by all means of transportation, and many could barely contain their emotions. "I'm not ashamed to say I was tearing up just like everybody else," former Secretary of State Colin Powell said. Georgia congressman John Lewis, who stood with Reverend Martin Luther King Jr. when he gave his "I Have a Dream" speech at the Lincoln Memorial in 1963, expressed deep feelings as well. "It's almost too much, too emotional," said Lewis. "Barack has lifted people. . . . Old people, young people, children, black and white. Look out on the Mall here. You can see it in their walk . . ."

President Obama had little time to relish his historical victory. America faced an unprecedented economic challenge. Billions of dollars had been allocated to keep America's banks from collapsing, but much more needed to be done. Thousands of people were losing their homes

Obama gives his inaugural address as a crowd of more than 1 million people watches from the National Mall in Washington, D.C. *(Courtesy of U.S. Dept. of Defense/Senior Master Sgt. Thomas Meneguin)*

and businesses were laying off more than a half a million workers each month.

The crisis was frightening, and most people responded by not purchasing items, such as cars and houses. This made the problem worse. With consumer spending down, companies had no choice but to cut back on the number of workers on their payrolls. The U.S. economy was in a vicious spiral that could lead to years of economic misery.

President Obama decided to take a bold step. Working with Congress he devised an economic recovery plan estimated to cost 800 billion dollars. The ambitious plan was a collection of spending initiatives and tax cuts. It aimed to create or preserve jobs by rebuilding the country's aging infrastructure, such as highways, bridges, and schools. To inspire hope in laid-off workers, the plan increased unemployment benefits, including subsidies for health insurance. Billions more was dedicated to help out the fifty states, many of which faced the prospect of laying off critical workers, including police, firemen, and teachers. Tax cuts accounted for almost a third of the plan. The thinking behind this aspect of the plan was if people had more money after paying taxes they would begin spending more.

President Obama's plan was supported by his own party. However, the Republican members of Congress rose up in opposition. They insisted the stimulus was a waste of tax-payer money. It was clear from his first days in office that the partisan political conflicts of the past decades were not over.

In a matter of days the Economic Recovery Act passed both houses of Congress. In the end only three Republican senators voted for it. Although this was a disappointment, President Obama was more concerned with getting the plan into action.

Managing to have his first major piece of legislation passed in such a short time was a major accomplishment. For example, President Ronald Reagan, who most historians consider to be one of the most effective presidents in working with Congress, did not have his first piece of major legisla-tion passed until late summer.

President Obama signed the bill on February 17, 2009, in Denver, Colorado, and the next day, in Mesa, Arizona, he unveiled a $75 billion plan to help millions of homeowners refinance their mortgages or avert foreclosure. He said he hoped the housing initiative would help reverse the economic slide that was "unraveling homeownership, the middle class, and the American dream itself."

Vice President Biden looks on as President Obama signs the $787 billion economic stimulus bill on February 17, 2009. *(Courtesy of AP Images)*

As the country moves forward to face these problems and others, it will do so under the leadership of one of the youngest and most active presidents in history. Only time will tell how successful Barack Obama has been in leading his country into a new, brighter future, but his election has changed American politics forever.

President Obama had acknowledged on Inauguration Day that repairing the U.S. economy would neither be quick, nor easy, but he promised to work toward solving these massive problems: "Today I say to you that the challenges we face are real. They are serious and they are many. They will not be met easily or in a short span of time. But know this, America—they will be met."

Timeline

1961 Born on August 4 in Honolulu, Hawaii.

1963 Father, a Kenyan also named Barack Obama, leaves
for Harvard; departure leads to parents' divorce.

1967 Moves with mother and her new husband, Lolo
Soetoro, to Indonesia.

1971 Returns to Hawaii to live with grandparents;
attends Punahou Academy; father visits from Kenya.

1979 Graduates from Punahou Academy; attends
Occidental College.

1981 Stepfather, Soetoro, travels to the U.S. to receive
treatment for a liver ailment; it's the last time the two
meet; switches to Columbia University.

1982 Father dies in a car accident at age forty-six.

1983 Graduates from Columbia University with a degree
in political science.

1985 Begins job as a community organizer in Chicago.

1987 Travels to Kenya for a monthlong visit with relatives.

1988 Enters Harvard Law School.

1989 Becomes the first African American president of
the *Harvard Law Review.*

1991 Begins dating Michelle Robinson; graduates from
Harvard and takes a job with a civil rights firm
in Chicago.

1992 Marries Michelle Robinson, also a lawyer, on
October 18.

1995 Publishes *Dreams from My Father: A Story of Race
and Inheritance*; mother, Ann, dies.

1996 Wins election for Illinois state senator.

1999 First daughter, Malia Ann, is born.

2000 Trounced in election for U.S. Senate by Bobby Rush.

2001 Second daughter, Natasha (nicknamed Sasha), is born.

2004 Gives stirring speech at Democratic National
Convention; wins election for U.S. Senate, becoming
the third black senator in history.

2005 Sworn in to the 109th Congress on January 4.

2006 Publishes second book, *The Audacity of Hope:
Thoughts on Reclaiming the American Dream.*

2007 Announces candidacy for U.S. president on
February 10.

2008 Defeats Hillary Clinton to become democratic presidential nominee; collapse of U.S. economy; death of grandmother; elected president of the United States over John McCain.

2009 Inaugurated as forty-fourth U.S. president; signs $787 billion economic recovery bill on February 17.

Sources

CHAPTER ONE: A Window to the World

p. 12, "My name comes . . ." Marlene Targ Brill,
Barack Obama: Working to Make a Difference
(Minneapolis: Millbrook Press, 2006), 9.

p. 19, "I could hardly believe . . ." Ibid., 18.

p. 21, "He would be . . ." Kristen Scharenberg and Kim
Barker, "The Not-So-Simple Story of Obama's Youth,"
Chicago Tribune, March 25, 2007.

p. 22, "If you want . . ." Brill, *Barack Obama: Working
to Make a Difference,* 19.

p. 22, "This is no . . ." Barack Obama, *Dreams from
My Father: A Story of Race and Inheritance* (New York:
Three Rivers Press, 2004), 48.

CHAPTER TWO: From Barry to Barack

p. 27, "This isn't school . . ." Obama, *Dreams from My
Father,* 58.

p. 29, "It's a fact . . ." Steve Dougherty, *Hopes and
Dreams: The Story of Barack Obama* (New York: Black
Dog & Leventhal 2007) 43.

p. 30-31, "He has been . . ." Obama, *Dreams from My Father,* 67.

p. 31, "Go now, before . . ." Ibid., 68.

p. 33, "I had to . . ." Joe Klein, "The Fresh Face," *Time Magazine,* October 15, 2006.

p. 33, "He had powers . . ." Amanda Ripley, "Obama's Ascent," *Time Magazine,* November 3, 2004.

p. 34, "Barry O'Bomber . . ." Scharenberg and Barker, "The Not-So-Simple Story of Obama's Youth."

p. 35, "He loved . . ." Brill, *Barack Obama: Working to Make a Difference,* 23.

p. 35, "I learned to . . ." Ripley, "Obama's Ascent."

p. 35, "Never had they . . ." Obama, *Dreams from My Father,* 89.

p. 36, "Junkie, pothead . . ." Brill, *Barack Obama,* 25.

p. 39, "Only a lack . . ." Dougherty, *Hopes and Dreams,* 58.

CHAPTER THREE: A Crumbling Community

p. 42, "There's nothing wrong . . ." Doughtery, *Hopes and Dreams,* 63.

p. 43, "It was in . . ." Barack Obama's official campaign Website, "Full Text of Senator Obama's Announcement," http://barackobama.com/2007/02/10/remarksof_senator _barack_obama_11.php.

p. 45-46, "He went from . . ." Brill, *Barack Obama,* 29.

p. 46, "People carried within . . ." Obama, *Dreams from My Father,* 190.

p. 46, "There was poetry . . ." Ibid.,190-191.

p. 46, "If you scratch . . ." Ibid., 208.

p. 46-47, "I can't say . . ." Ibid., 212.

p. 48, "I was just . . ." Ibid., 219.

p. 49, "We need to . . ." Ibid., 222.

p. 49, "The change comes . . ." Ibid., 233.

p. 51, "Obama's army," Ibid., 238.

p. 51, "I changed as . . ." Ibid., 242.

p. 52, "The people were . . ." Ibid., 259.

p. 52, "People came . . ." Ibid., 265.

p. 53, "Ain't nobody gonna . . ." Ibid., 276.

p. 55, "We've got a lot . . ." Ibid., 282.

CHAPTER FOUR: Spirits of the Past

p. 58, "Welcome home," Obama, *Dreams from My Father,* 306.

p. 59, "You take good . . ." Ibid., 307.

p. 60, "They've been lost . . ." Ibid.

p. 60, "My son," Ibid., 316.

p. 61, "Sometimes I have . . ." Ibid., 320.

p. 61, "You must learn . . ." Ibid., 337.

p. 63, "A pride of..." Ibid., 356.

p. 63, "There's your ordinary . . ." Ibid., 369.

p. 64, "She says she . . ." Ibid., 374.

p. 64, "She understands that . . ." Ibid., 377.

p. 67-68, "He says that . . ." Ibid., 388.

p. 68, "I saw that . . ." Ibid., 430.

CHAPTER FIVE: Hope and Ambitions

p. 70, "On first impression . . ." Brill, *Barack Obama*, 32.

p. 72, "one of the two . . ." Dougherty, *Hopes and Dreams,* 77-78.

p. 72, "The law also . . ." Obama, *Dreams from My Father,* 437.

p. 74, "there were uncles . . ." Barack Obama, *The Audacity of Hope: Thoughts on Reclaiming the American Dream* (New York: Crown Publishers, 2006), 330.

p. 74, "She said . . ." Dougherty, *Hopes and Dreams,* 78.

p. 79, "We have a . . ." Obama, *The Audacity of Hope,* 2.

p. 80, "a rough stew . . ." Ibid., 49.

p. 81, "In the faces . . ." Ibid., 50-51.

p. 84, "the sort of . . ." Dougherty, *Hopes and Dreams,* 28.

CHAPTER SIX: A Rising Star

p. 86, "shouldn't necessarily count . . ." Doughtery, *Hopes and Dreams,* 88.

p. 86, "My ten volunteers . . ." Obama, *The Audacity of Hope,* 6.

p. 87, "I tried my . . ." Ibid.

p. 89, "Yes, we can," Brill, *Barack Obama,* 39.

p. 89-90, "All I had . . ." Obama, *The Audacity of Hope,* 211.

p. 90, "People call me . . ." David Mendell, "Obama Banks on Credentials, Charisma: Another in a Series of Sunday Profiles on Candidates for the U.S. Senate in the March 16 Primary," *Chicago Tribune,* metro section, January 25, 2004.

p. 90, "He jumped back . . ." Dougherty, *Hopes and Dreams,* 34.

p. 90, "Well, I don't know . . . Ibid.

p. 91, "Just don't . . ." Ibid., 75.

p. 92, "I say tonight . . ." Brill, *Barack Obama,* 8.

p. 92, "He is without . . ." Mendell, "Obama Banks on Credentials, Charisma: Another in a Series of Sunday Profiles on Candidates for the U.S. Senate in the March 16 Primary."

p. 94, "I felt like . . ." Obama, *The Audacity of Hope,* 19.

p. 94, "Great Black Hope," Brill, *Barack Obama,* 41.

p. 96, "Who, I wondered . . ." Obama, *The Audacity of Hope,* 44.

p. 96, "It's like drinking . . ." Ibid., 71.

p. 99, "Whenever I write . . ." Ibid., 48.

p. 101, "A dumb war . . ." Ibid., 295.

p. 102, "He's a hero . . ." Jeff Zekeny, "Kenyans Welcome is Heavy with Hope," *Chicago Tribune,* August 29, 2007.

CHAPTER SEVEN: Together We Can

p. 104, "Obama for President," Dougherty, *Hopes and Dreams,* 34.

p. 104, "He's ready . . ." Ibid.

p. 105, "We originally scheduled," Ibid., 9, 11.

p. 106, "Sometimes a book . . ." Ibid., 13.

p. 106, "Run, Barack, Run . . ." Ibid., 20.

p. 107, "Whatever we once . . ." Obama, *The Audacity of Hope,* 218.

p. 107, "War hero against . . ." Dougherty, *Hopes and Dreams,* 108.

p. 109, "There's something . . ." Ibid., 108.

p. 109, "It's a much . . ." Brian Charlton, "Obama Set to Make '08 Call in Isles." *Honolulu Star Bulletin,* December 20, 2006.

p. 112, "Few obstacles can . . ." Barack Obama's official campaign Web site, "Full Text of Senator Obama's Announcement," http://barackobama.com/2007/02/10/.

p. 113, "Beneath all the . . ." Ibid.

CHAPTER EIGHT: From Dream to Reality

p. 124, "It has been . . ." Evan Thomas, "The Final Days," *Newsweek*, November 7, 2008, http://www.newsweek.com/id/168017/page/7.

p. 124, "I'm not ashamed . . ." Emily Friedman, "Black Leaders React to Obama's Inauguration," *ABC News*, January 20, 2009, http://abcnews.go.com/Politics/Inauguration/Story?id=6682054&page=1.

P, 125, "It's almost too much . . ." David Remnick, "The President's Hero," *New Yorker*, February 2, 2009, http://www.newyorker.com/talk/comment/2009/02/02/090202taco_talk_remnick.

p. 126, "unraveling homeownership . . ." Christi Parsons and Peter Nicholas, "Obama Unveils Mortgage Relief Plan," *Los Angeles Times*, February 19, 2009, http://www.latimes.com/news/nationworld/washingtondc/la-na-obama-housing19-2009feb19,0,4326570.story.

p. 127, "Today I say to you . . ." Barack Obama, "President Barack Obama's Inaugural Address," White House Blog, January 21, 2009, http://www.whitehouse.gov/blog/inaugural-address//.

Bibliography

Barack Obama official campaign Web site. "Full Text of Senator Barack Obama's Announcement." http://www.barackobama.com/2007/02/10/remarksof_senator_barack_obama_11.php

———. "Just Because Someone Writes It Does Not Make It True." http://www.barackobama.com/2007/02/19/just_because_someone_writes_it.php

Brill, Marlene Targ. *Barack Obama: Working to Make a Difference.* Minneapolis: Millbrook Press, 2006.

Charlton, Brian. "Obama Set to Make '08 Call in Isles." *Honolulu Star Bulletin,* December 20, 2006, News section.

Dorning, Mike. "Forget Sleep it's Time for Fundraising." *Chicago Tribune.* January 23, 2007, News section, Chicagoland final edition.

Dorning, Mike, and Christi Parsons. "Inside Obama's Inner Circle." *Chicago Tribune,* January 14, 2007, News section, Chicagoland final edition.

Dougherty, Steve. *Hopes and Dreams: The Story of*

Barack Obama. New York: Black Dog & Leventhal, 2007.

Hopefund. "Yes We Can Overview." Hopefund. http://hopefundamerica.com/yeswecan.

Klein, Joe. "The Fresh Face." *Time,* October 15, 2006.

Mendell, David. "Obama Banks on Credentials, Charisma Series: Another in a Series of Sunday Profiles on Candidates for the U.S. Senate in the March 16 Primary." *Chicago Tribune,* January 25, 2004, Metro section, Chicago final edition.

Obama, Barack. *Dreams from My Father: A Story of Race and Inheritance.* New York: Three Rivers Press, 2004.

———. *The Audacity of Hope: Thoughts on Reclaiming the American Dream.* New York: Crown Publishers, 2006.

Parsons, Christi. "Obama Aides Claim Surge of Support." *Chicago Tribune,* January 18, 2007, News section, Chicago final edition.

Remnick, David. "Testing the Waters." *New Yorker,* October 30, 2006, Final edition.

Ripley, Amanda. "Obama's Ascent." *Time,* November 3, 2004. http://time.com/time/magazine/article.

Scharenberg, Kristen and Kim Barker. "The Not-So-Simple Story of Obama's Youth." *Chicago Tribune,* March 25, 2007, Sunday Times section, Chicagoland final edition.

Sheridan, Michael, and Sarah Baxter. "Secrets of Obama Family Unlocked." *Australian,* January 29, 2007, Sunday Times section.

Steinhauer, Jennifer. "In Hawaii, Clues from Barack Obama's Origins." *International Herald Tribune,* March 17, 2007, Regions section.

Zeleny, Jeff. "Kenyans Welcome is Heavy with Hope." *Chicago Tribune,* August 29, 2007, News section, Chicagoland final edition.

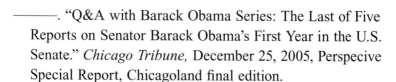 **Political Profiles**

———. "Q&A with Barack Obama Series: The Last of Five
Reports on Senator Barack Obama's First Year in the U.S.
Senate." *Chicago Tribune,* December 25, 2005, Perspecive
Special Report, Chicagoland final edition.
———. "Q&A with Michelle Obama Series: The Last of
Five Reports on Senator Barack Obama's First Year in
the U.S. Senate." *Chicago Tribune,* December 25,
2005, Perspecive Special Report, Chicagoland
final edition.
———. "The First Time Around: Senator Barack Obama's
Freshman Year Series: The Last of Five Reports on
Senator Barack Obama's First Year in the U.S. Senate."
Chicago Tribune, December 25, 2005, Perspective
Special Report, Chicagoland final edition.

Web sites

www.barackobama.com
The official Web site of Barack Obama. Features information on Obama's programs, a frequently updated blog, and links to other Obama supporting sites, including Obama's Facebook page.

www.whitehouse.gov
The official Web site of the U.S. President. Contains up-to-date information on the President's actions and plans, as well as comprehensive data on all bills signed by the President.

www.democrats.org
The Web site of Obama's political party, the Democrats. Features information on the Democratic party, its members, and ways to get involved in the community.

www.rnc.org
The Web site of the Republican party. Features information on the Republican party, its members, and ways to get involved in the community.

Index